THE AMERICAN ROAD TO

WORLD PEACE

The American Road to World Peace

by

Sir Alfred Zimmern

*Emeritus Professor of International Relations
in the University of Oxford*

*Co-Founder and Director of
The Geneva School of International Studies
(1924–39)*

EST·1852

NEW YORK
E. P. Dutton & Company, Inc.
1953

TO

OUR STUDENTS

WHEREVER THEY ARE

◇◇◇

ACKNOWLEDGMENTS

THANKS are due to the following for permission to cite extracts from books or other publications with which they are concerned:

to former Secretary of State Cordell Hull and to his publishers the Macmillan Company, New York, in respect to *The Memoirs of Cordell Hull*, copyright 1948.

to E. P. Dutton & Co., Inc. in respect to *The Way of the Free* by Stefan Osusky, 1951.

to Henry Holt & Co., in respect to *Democratic Ideas and Reality* by Sir Halford J. Mackinder, 1942 and to *A Diplomatic History of the United States* by Samuel Flagg Bemis, 1937.

to Houghton Mifflin & Co., in respect to *The Gathering Storm, The Grand Alliance* and *The Hinge of Fate* by the Rt. Hon. Winston S. Churchill, 1948, 1950 and 1951, to *The Intimate Papers of Colonel House*, edited by Charles Seymour, 1926-28, and to *Private Papers* by Arthur Vandenberg, 1952.

to former Ambassador Philip G. Jessup, to the Oxford University Press and to the Council of Foreign Relations in respect to *Elihu Root*, 1941 and *International Security*, 1935.

to Professor McGeorge Bundy, and to Harper & Brothers in respect to On Active Service in *Peace and War* by Henry L. Stimson and McGeorge Bundy, 1948.

to Mr. Albert Shaw, jr., and Dr. Roger Shaw in respect to *The Messages and Papers of Woodrow Wilson, with editorial notes and an introduction* by Albert Shaw and an analytical index, New York, The Review of Reviews Corporation, 1924.

to Harper Brothers in respect to *Roosevelt and Hopkins* by Robert Sherwood, 1948, and *Speaking Frankly* by former Secretary of State James F. Byrnes, 1947.

Acknowledgments

to Mrs. Katherine Marshall and Tupper & Love, Inc. 1946, Atlanta, Ga. in respect to her book *Together*.

to the Council on Foreign Relations in respect to articles in *Foreign Affairs* by Mr. Allen W. Dulles and Dr. J. R. Oppenheimer.

to Little, Brown and Co., in respect to *United States Foreign Policy* by Walter Lippman, 1943.

to the New York University Press in respect to *The Annual Review of United Nations Affairs*.

to Messrs. F. W. Cheshire, Melbourne & London, in respect to *The Workshop of Security* by Paul Hasluck, 1948 and

to the Royal Institute of International Affairs in respect to their publications *The Problem of Atomic Energy* and *Atlantic Alliance* (1948 and 1952).

TABLE OF CONTENTS

Preface
13

PART I

BEFORE THE UNITED NATIONS

SECTION I
The Warning of a Great Geographer

SECTION II
America, the Citadel of Freedom

SECTION III
Europe

Europe

SECTION IV
1914

SECTION V
Woodrow Wilson and Elihu Root

PREFACE

THIS book is the result of many years of observation and reflection, dating back to World War I. Its outline took shape within a few months of our return to this country, early in 1947, after an absence of eight years, but it was actually written under the impact of the events of 1952, when the election of a new President seemed to make it inevitable that the United Nations Organization and the policy of the United States government toward it would be brought under fresh review.

If some readers may be inclined to think that I have pitched my hopes for American democracy too high, I can only say that I have written out of the daily experience of life in two of those smaller towns which are the seedbeds of American public opinion and best exemplify the working of American institutions and the American way of life.

It was my original intention to conclude the book with a section on American education in its relation to the understanding of world affairs. This subject is closely bound up with the suggestions put forward in the later chapters for the exercise of American leadership in developing the full possibilities of the United Nations Charter. But I came to the conclusion that I could not include such a discussion in the present volume without adding unduly to its bulk and distracting attention from the thread of its main political argument. So these pages, as they stand, aim at being a contribution to political science and the book on education will follow.

To any of my British compatriots into whose hands this volume may fall I would like to say that, should it be published in the British Commonwealth, my wish would be to write an introductory section bringing the British position, as I see it today, into line with our tradition in the past and with recent social and constitutional developments.

Preface

My thanks are due to our many friends and neighbors in Hartford and Springfield who have enriched our life and nourished our thoughts during the years when this book was in preparation. Special acknowledgments are due to the staffs of the Public Libraries in Springfield and Hartford and to the authorities of the Connecticut State Library, the Hartford Seminary Foundation, and Trinity College for their unfailing courtesy and helpfulness.

This volume was thought out and has reached written form in constant co-operation with my wife, as has been the case in all our educational work. It is impossible to separate her part in it from mine.

A. Z.

Springfield, Mass.

PART I
Before The United Nations

Prometheus stole the mechanical arts and fire with them,
and gave them to man. Thus man had the support of life,
but political wisdom he had not. . . . Having no art of
government, they evil entreated one another and were in
process of destruction.

PLATO, PROTAGORAS, 321-2

THE WARNING OF A GREAT GEOGRAPHER

SECTION I

THE WARNING OF A GREAT GEOGRAPHER

"Who rules East Europe commands the Heartland:
Who rules the Heartland commands the World Island:
Who rules the World Island commands the World."

CHAPTER 1: *The Three Islands*

IN a lecture delivered in 1904 before the Royal Geographical Society of Great Britain a young Oxford teacher of the subject, Mr. H. J. Mackinder (as he then was) called upon his colleagues to look at the planet with fresh eyes.

That lecture, entitled "The Geographical Pivot of History," marked the opening of a new era in the study of political geography and of the art of world strategy which is so closely related to it.

The originality of Mackinder's contribution consisted above all in the breadth and sweep of his approach. Fixing his gaze first on the Eastern Hemisphere, comprising the "Continents" of Europe, Asia, and Africa, he showed that it was a single great land mass surrounded by ocean water. He called this land mass "the World

19

Island." He drew attention to the fact that, from the beginning of recorded history, the World Island had been the chief repository of political power on the planet and the scene of what had generally been considered the most important events in the history of mankind—in particular, of the rise and fall of the "Empires" and other organizations of power which had dominated and largely molded the life and the social and economic conditions of the peoples inhabiting what was known as "the Old World."

Set over against the Old World, with its abundant population and resources, both natural and industrialized, there was, Mackinder pointed out, another island, the second largest on the planet, the island of the Americas, situated in the Western ocean. This second island weighed less in the scales of power than the first and, even though the northern section of it was organized on sound political lines, this disparity was likely to continue for an indefinite period. Speaking at a time when the supremacy of Great Britain, based on the resources of an island very much smaller than the two already mentioned, had been an established political fact in world politics for a century past, he sounded a clear note of warning. He reminded his fellow countrymen that the distribution of power in the early twentieth-century world was dangerously unstable and that British and American (not to speak of Australasian) statesmen ought to reckon seriously with the possibility that the resources of the World Island might at any time fall into the hands of a single power controlling the inaccessible region which he named the Heartland. Such a power would be enabled to outbuild the British Navy and then, having made itself supreme in the Old World, to proceed in its own time to secure domination over the Americas.

This warning fell upon American ears at a formative moment in American strategic thinking and has exercised a great and lasting influence during the last two generations on those successively responsible for the defense of the United States. Indeed, if it can be claimed for any one man that he originated the concept of the Atlantic Community—a concept which so boldly challenges the plain facts of physical geography — that man is Mackinder.

MACKINDER was, by training and profession, a geographer—a geographer who, by reflecting more deeply than his colleagues on the conclusions to be drawn from his special knowledge, became a strategist with counsels of value for general staffs and, through them, for statesmen. But he was not a constructive *political* thinker. Nor indeed did he ever claim to be one. So far as public affairs were concerned, he regarded it as his duty to keep his fellow countrymen and the peoples of the English-speaking world constantly aware of what he called the "realities" of world politics, stark realities underlying practical politics of any kind, democratic or otherwise. The primary purpose of political activity, he always maintained, as Aristotle had maintained before him, was to ensure life—the survival of the citizens and the state or community to which they belonged. Only after that had been ensured was it legitimate for public men to spend time and thought on the organization of the "good life," that is to say, on arrangements in which the survival of the state could be taken for granted.

In the days when Mackinder was setting forth these views at Oxford, in the first decade of the century, nothing seemed less likely to the young men who listened to him than that their careers would be set in an age in which the civilization they had inherited from the Victorian era would be sharply challenged and the very continuance of ordered life in the small island of Great Britain placed in jeopardy. He himself lived to see the cloud, which he had discerned when it was no bigger than a man's hand, darkening the whole planet, but he had passed away before the gravest threat to the survival of our civilization—the acquisition by the rulers of the Heartland of control over the instruments of atomic power—had become a grim and ever-present reality for the responsible statesmen and peoples of the free world.

AMERICA, THE CITADEL OF FREEDOM

◇◇

SECTION II

AMERICA, THE CITADEL OF FREEDOM

"America is more than a country: it is a state of mind."

CHAPTER 3: *What is the Free World?*

WHAT do we mean when we speak of the free world?

We mean a world in which the relations of men to one another are neighborly and helpful rather than unkind, suspicious, and either actually or potentially hostile. We mean a world in which this friendly spirit is the predominant note in all the various social groupings which together make up organized and civilized life— beginning with the family and extending, through the local community, the township, and the county, and the state or province, to the organization representing the nation or people as a whole. We mean a world in which men and women are not too busy or too self-centered to rise to an occasion, like the Good Samaritan, and in which those to whose directions we conform, the Caesars to whom we pay our taxes and render obedience in other ways, themselves acknowledge that they are subject to a higher authority, the authority of conscience. A free world is a world in which men willingly co-operate with the law and in which the law itself is felt to be, in the classic words of Justice Holmes, "the witness and external deposit of our moral life."

CHAPTER 4: *Is there Such a Free World?*

IS there such a free world? Or is it a mere creation of fancy, the product of the kind of wishful thinking which has brought so much bitter disillusionment to the American and other peoples in recent years?

Yes, there is such a free world. Americans, with instinctive reticence, may be inclined to shrink from admitting it, but it is plain enough to those who, having begun life elsewhere, have come to live in the spacious land of responsibility and opportunity that opens out behind the Statue of Liberty. And it is openly proclaimed to all on shipboard when the first official representative of the United States, no arrogant jack-in-office but a man of friendly countenance and easy approach, calls upon citizens to stand on one side and all the other passengers to assemble separately.

There is a fundamental difference between the relation of men to one another in the larger World Island and in North America. In the Old World men are usually described as *subjects*. In the New World they are *citizens*. This is the right designation for free men—free in law and free within themselves in their inner life.

CHAPTER 5: *Where Are the Boundaries of Freedom?*

WHEN the Fathers of the Constitution wrote into the Preamble that their purpose was to "secure the blessings of liberty to ourselves and our posterity," they did not fully realize that they could only achieve this object by fortifying liberty all the world over. It was enough for them to secure free institutions in thirteen small settlements lying aloof from the storm centers of world politics.

Yet, as it has turned out, the people of the United States cannot secure the blessings of liberty for themselves without communicating their ideals and their experience to the other peoples of the world and giving them vigorous encouragement to follow on the path that they staked out for themselves in 1787. As we read the Declaration of Independence today, in the light of all that has been achieved under its inspiration, can we conceive that its author and his co-signatories would have shrunk from admitting the world-wide applicability of its doctrines? For in 1776 it was springtime and those who were banded together in the struggle for freedom in North America sensed that far more than local issues were at stake. When the spirit of freedom is abroad, it sets habit and custom at naught and overleaps the boundaries of ancient states. At such moments men live in the present and the future, not in the past.

CHAPTER 6: *The Past History of Freedom*

BUT has freedom indeed a past? Had it a past in 1776? Has it a past in the Old World today? Has freedom taken root anywhere in the world except in North America?

To have asked such a question fifty years ago, at the time when a great English scholar was compiling the materials for what was designed to be the definitive study of freedom up to that time, would have been considered distinctly out of place. But in these years of nightmare, when so many Old World thinkers are discouraged through lack of faith or allow themselves to be inhibited by fear, and when talented writers seek solace in minor—not to say frivolous—themes, the question is at least worth asking.

The *idea* of freedom originated in the Old World. Jefferson did not evolve it out of his inner consciousness. But is its history, as we can survey it today, more than the record of an idea? Is freedom firmly planted in the consciousness of the Old World peoples? Has it taken root in institutions which keep it alive and potent in the minds of each passing generation, as the Declaration and the Constitution constantly nourish and invigorate the people of the United States? How has it come about that large sections of the voting population in countries of ancient culture, like France and Italy, have embraced doctrines which abjure freedom? And how is it that such doctrines have cast their spell in particular over so many of those who consider themselves "intellectuals," upon whom the rest of the community has been accustomed to rely for the maintenance of standards of honesty in the realm of the mind? Has there been, in the language of a French writer, a widespread resort to "treason" on the part of European intellectuals?

Before we pass judgment too hastily on this matter, let us bear in mind that on the Continent of Europe freedom has never at any time been more than a minority cause, maintaining itself precariously in the face of massive opposition—an opposition which has today assembled forces, social, economic, and psychological, as well as political, that are more formidable, at least in outward appearance, than ever before. Englishmen have never known subjection. They have never known what it is to be deprived of what to us is as natural as the air we breathe. But to a large part of the population of Europe freedom was unknown before 1918 and, when the great prize had been gained, it was withdrawn before the peoples concerned had accustomed themselves to it and learned to make full use of it in their institutions. Never will the writer forget the last conversation that he had—it was in the summer of 1938—with a Czech friend, the curator of the library of President Masaryk. "What we have been living through since 1918," he said sadly, "seems to me now, as I look back, like an idyl, a short interval after a long darkness, and before we are plunged into darkness again." The librarian and his fine circle of friends, who did so much to keep freedom alive in the minds and hearts of their fellow countrymen, did not live to come out of the long darkness. It will be for a new generation of Europeans to transform freedom from a political and spiritual concept to a constitutional reality, so that it can be handed on, as Americans hand it on, as an inheritance which men take for granted.

CHAPTER 7: *The Dilemma of Free Government*

THERE is an inescapable dilemma which freedom has had to face in every age until the present—a dilemma on which Montesquieu already laid his finger. This is the dilemma.

On the one hand, freedom can never be the constant inspiration of a great power, for inevitably Great Powers set up conditions in which freedom withers and disappears.

On the other hand, freedom cannot survive as an influence in the political life of the world unless it is more than a mere idea—unless it becomes a constitutional reality: and it cannot become that unless it is backed by material power enabling it to survive and to organize itself in actual institutions.

As the great Christian thinker, Blaise Pascal, put it in words often cited but still insufficiently heeded by many Christians: "Justice without Force is impotent: Force without Justice is tyrannical. . . . It is necessary therefore to put together Justice and Force and so ensure that that which is just shall be strong and that that which is strong shall be just."

This dilemma, hitherto insoluble, has now been resolved by the United States, the first free Great Power in history, a new type of Great Power.

CHAPTER 8: *The United States as a Free Society*

FREEDOM finds its natural home in small communities where men can practice neighborly relations toward one another without the ever-present danger of interference by unfriendly forces from outside. Such conditions have been rare in the Old World. They have existed in small secluded areas of cultivable land amid the tangled mountains of Greece, in similar areas in the valleys of the Swiss Alps, and in certain fortunate islands, notably Great Britain and Iceland. As Wordsworth proclaimed when Napoleon was at the height of his glory, freedom has "two voices, one of the sea, one of the mountains, each a mighty voice." But not mighty in the sense of the massive power of great land armies.

Freedom has found a natural home in North America because the United States is not a Great Power in the Old World sense of the term. It is not a "sovereign state." The United States, as the plural form attests, is a union of forty-eight self-governing communities, each of them subdivided into equally self-governing counties and townships. Such a union is quite different from the centralized organization of a European "great power." It is indeed, primarily and in essence, not political at all: it is *social*. It is not a "body politic," which *in itself* is no more than a contrivance or, as one writer has recently called it, a "device." It is a *body social*, an organic whole compacted of the essence of all its manifold and variegated parts—*how* organic is never better manifested than in the nationwide process of convergence and concentration which characterizes an election year.

How is it then that the United States has become the most powerful country in the world, more powerful than the realm of any Caesar or Czar, ancient or modern, while remaining *at the same time* a community, a body social, preserving the neighborly qualities of its origin?

It is because, owing to a course of events to which there is no parallel in history—one might say, through a blessed dispensation of Providence—the original settlers in North America founded their homes and established their way of life, on lines more sound and "natural" than those of the greater part of the Old World, in small self-governing communities, and because, having an expanse of practically virgin territory beyond their farther borders, they were able to extend their settlements and their characteristic way of life little by little until they reached the Western ocean thousands of miles away. Thus, without realizing the unique character of their work, they brought into existence a single body social and this, in due time, established such governmental arrangements as were needed for common purposes, including, of course, the conduct of external relations.

Thus the United States has become a Great Power, but a Great Power different in quality and texture from any Great Power hitherto known to the Old World, with the exception of Athens during the short half-century of her political greatness.

That is why Americans have the right to feel that the history of freedom lies before them and not behind them.

EUROPE

SECTION III

EUROPE

"Why can't you Europeans all get together?"
—Any GI to any European.
"European history is for Americans to understand
and for Europeans to ponder over."

CHAPTER 9: *Europe a Conundrum for Americans*

THE American people has now become very much mixed up with the politics of the Eastern Hemisphere and particularly with Europe, the region which, from the discovery of gunpowder in the fourteenth century until quite recently, was the center of political power on the planet.

It took a long time and cost them a deep inner struggle before Americans overcame their reluctance to play a part in the affairs of the Old World, upon which so many of them, or of their ancestors, had turned their backs with relief. In the eyes of European statesmen, the United States joined the ranks of the Great Powers at least as early as the Spanish-American War, if not in the days of Grover Cleveland; but it was close on half a century later before the realization of this fact was brought home to the nation as a whole, irrespective of internal differences. The moment of final decision was December 7, 1941. The attack on Pearl Harbor not only stirred all Americans in a common impulse of self-defense but opened their eyes to the power vacuum which,

35

through excessive trustfulness, they had left open to be occupied by enemies of freedom in the Pacific, the greatest of the world's oceans.

Since then Americans have had to concern themselves closely with Europe and European power politics. Yet they have continued to feel uneasy about this relationship because they are aware that they are on unfamiliar ground. One manifestation of this uneasiness has been the recurring tendency to think in terms of pre-Pearl Harbor policies; but these have only to be looked at closely to be revealed as no longer in the realm of practical politics. Another manifestation is the desire to see Europe through American spectacles and to picture its peoples as on the eve of a movement of union similar to that of the American people of the Thirteen States in 1787. This would seem to be the natural, indeed the inevitable, course for the peoples of Western Europe to take in view of their defenselessness against the military power of the Soviet Union. Yet in the years which have elapsed since the end of fighting in Europe, the movement toward "European Union," though it has made some progress, has not developed on the lines that many Americans expected. The federal formula, which appeals to Americans at first sight, has turned out to be too simple to meet the case. It involves difficulties which European statesmen, with the best will in the world, have been unable to overcome— if indeed one is justified in describing the statesmen of any one country across the water as European. They are certainly not "European" in the sense in which those who speak in the name of the United States are American.

Before we come to close grips with American policy in world affairs, let us first direct our gaze across the Atlantic and take a good look at this "Europe," seeking to explain why, inhabited though it is by human beings endowed with reason and a high average intelligence, their behavior, as seen from the opposite side of the water, presents such a conundrum.

It is not easy to summarize Europe within the limits of a few pages, but, if one has lived on both sides of the Atlantic, one can at least emphasize certain elements some knowledge of which is essential for Americans wishing to understand that continent.

36

CHAPTER 10: *The Double Heritage of Greece*

TO interpret Europe one cannot avoid going back to ancient history, to Greece and Rome. This means an excursion into a distant past, but a past which, in both cases, is still very much alive.

When we speak of Greece, we mean a particular period in the history of that small Balkan country, a period covering the life of the free Greek republics in their bloom from about 800 B.C. to about 250 B.C., some time after they had lost their independence and when the momentum of their former freedom had died down.

The Greeks of that period were the most creative people known to history. Most things in which persons with live minds on either side of the Atlantic are interested go back to the Greeks. In two fields in particular they showed their genius—in the field of culture and in the field of politics. In the field of culture they were the pioneers of all the various branches of knowledge and the fine arts that are now used as educational material in our schools, colleges, and universities. Moreover, they were not only pioneers, but also co-ordinators. They not only discovered or thought out this material for the first time, but they also co-ordinated it, assembling it in its right place in the scheme of human knowledge.

CHAPTER 11: *Genuine and Artificial Culture*

AFTER the age of Greek creativeness passed away, this heritage of "culture" was handed on to other peoples, chiefly through the medium of the Romans, and became an inseparable part of the intellectual and artistic life of the peoples of Europe. The fact that this culture reached them indirectly and at second hand

37

tended at first to create a social cleavage, which took different forms in different countries, between those who were "learned" or "educated" and the rest of the population. But, speaking generally, the European peoples had enough native vigor to withstand what was weakening and artificial in an imported culture. In the case of France, a Latin country, the assimilation of the influence of Greece and Rome into the everyday life of all sections of the French people, peasants and town dwellers alike, has been so harmonious as to constitute a sociological model. In England, the only other instance which can be cited in this brief account, the growth of the national culture encountered greater difficulties, as can be seen in the twofold structure, at once Anglo-Saxon and Latin, of the English language. But these had been surmounted before the Elizabethan Age: one has only to mention the names of Shakespeare and Milton, upon whom the influence of Greece and Rome, so different in each case, left so deep a mark.

A similar form of national integration, at a somewhat earlier stage in the process of assimilation, has been taking place in the relationship between "European culture" as a whole and that of the American people. This has such an important bearing on political relationships, and indeed on the whole problem of mutual understanding and assured peace between the peoples concerned, that it cannot be passed over in this analysis.

Culture is a quality of individuals. We rightly speak of a man or woman as a "cultured person." What do we mean by that? We do not mean a person who is erudite, or who speaks several languages, or who possesses the social graces. These may, or may not, be, adjuncts of culture in particular individuals. The true function of culture is to help men and women *to find themselves*. And the true function of culture, when applied to a social group or nation, is to help these equally to develop to the full their social consciousness.

This is what has been happening in the case of the American people now for many generations past, and very markedly during the last fifty years. Though the view that culture is an embellishment reserved for the chosen few is still to be found in some circles, the independence and originality of American culture, proclaimed by Emerson in his Phi Beta Kappa Address of 1837, is generally recognized and the number of those who hold a contrary view is dwindling away. Much, however, still remains to be done before American culture, in its specific quality, is generally understood in Europe, even in "educated" circles.

CHAPTER 12: *Greek Political Creativeness*

IN the field of politics the transmission of the Greek heritage encountered very different conditions. Here, too, the Greeks broke completely fresh ground. In their small communities of cultivators and craftsmen they *discovered* methods for the conduct of public affairs which are now recognized to be the right methods. They originated the concept and worked out the technique of constitutional democracy; and the memory of this achievement was perpetuated by a series of thinkers: Socrates, Plato, and Aristotle, who discussed the problems and threshed out many of the issues involved in the working of a free society—in particular, the relationship between Politics and Ethics and the question of the nature of Justice and Freedom as political and social concepts.

CHAPTER 13: *The Long Winter of the Social Sciences*

HAD the fourth century B.C. pursued a normal course, the political concepts and the practical experience thus made available would in due time have influenced neighboring free peoples in the same way as Greek "culture." But, unfortunately, after the third century B.C. there were virtually no free peoples left in the Eastern Mediterranean area. The Macedonian conquest of Greece was the forerunner of an age of other conquests in which monarchs, for whom freedom was a word without meaning, were pitted against one another. Eventually one single power emerged victorious and supreme over the whole Mediterranean basin and the greater part of Europe, the power based on the Italian city of Rome.

As a result of the extinction of freedom, not only did the institutions originated by the Greeks disappear, but the greater part of the edifice of thought which they had constructed crumbled away also. The political and social sciences, in particular, went into hibernation in a prolonged winter which lasted till the seventeenth century. It is true that "cultured" Romans, such as Cicero, read the Greek books and made play with the ideas they found in them. But the Romans were not gifted with intellectual insight and the result of their intrusion into the realm of Greek political and social theory was to involve the subject in a confusion which has even today not yet been fully cleared away. Thus, as we shall see later on, there are deep-lying differences of opinion at the present time among the members of the United Nations, or rather between their experts, as to the meaning of some of the terms in most common use in the discussion of world affairs.

CHAPTER 14: *The Roman Empire*

THE Roman Empire dates from the moment when, after a period of civil war between various generals and politicians, Julius Caesar set at naught the old Roman constitutional system based on the Senate and people of that city and its surrounding territory. In the absence of the device of representation, a political invention reserved for a later time, that system was already clearly inadequate for the government of the Mediterranean basin. Caesar, who had been constitutionally invested with the title of Dictator—an office tenable for six months in times of grave emergency—made known his intention to prolong his tenure of office and to assume the insignia of a King. On March 15 (the "Ides of March") of the year 44 B.C. he was struck down and killed in the Senate House by a band of outraged champions of the Roman Republic. Another period of civil war ensued until, in 31 B.C., after a naval battle off the coast of Albania, a young nephew of Caesar found himself in possession of the supreme power. This marked the effective beginning of the Roman Empire.

The Roman Empire still looms so large in the mind of Europeans and has left such important traces in the institutions of most of them that, without entering into a full analysis, it is necessary to make some main points very clear.

The new ruler, who assumed the name of Augustus, was a "cultured" Roman of a prudent and conservative disposition. He therefore did all that he could to conceal the fact that he had become the possessor of supreme power. The old republican forms were preserved in Rome and the relations between the ruling "city" and her "allied" and subject states were left unchanged. Two centuries and more had passed before, by an imperial edict of the year A.D. 212, the old distinctions between "Romans," "Latins," "Italians," and "Provincials" were abolished and all free (i.e. nonslave) inhabitants of the Empire became Roman "citizens." But by that time the term "citizen" had long since lost its meaning, and even the shadow of its meaning. For the Roman Empire was in no sense a constitutional structure. At times, as under Augustus, it was a benevolent monarchy; at other times it was a tyranny, especially when emperors were being set up and deposed by the armed forces; and at all times, insofar as it was a going concern, it was a bureaucracy.

41

IT is in its capacity as a bureaucracy that the Roman Empire survives in modern Europe; for the government of its vast territories could not be carried on without a framework of general principles embodied in administrative rules. Augustus was wise enough to see this and to seek expert advice for this purpose. The available experts were "cultured" attorneys who had studied political science, not indeed in the writings of the classical age but in the form in vogue at that time, the so-called Stoic philosophy. The Stoics inherited the intellectual clarity and penetration of the Greeks of the great age, but they had lost all contact with the spirit of democracy. They and their pupils were what we should call today an elite. Their ideal was not one of good citizenship but of the "self-sufficient" individual, humane in temper but aloof from the vulgar crowd. It was these philosophically minded consultants who, over the generations, supplied the Roman administrative machine with the principles of what became known as the "Civil Law." The scattered elements of their labors were eventually drawn together in the shape of a regular code; this took place at Constantinople after the fall of the Western Roman Empire, at the instance of the Emperor Justinian, in the years A.D. 529-33.

This code was rediscovered by scholars after the Dark Ages and became a principal object of study in the twelfth century in the young and vigorous University of Bologna, though the social conditions to which its rules related had long since passed away. The zealous antiquarianism of the Bologna professors, and of their colleagues in other seats of learning, gave rise to a movement in the cultured circles of the day which resulted in the adoption of these Roman rules and principles as the groundwork of practically all the emerging states of Europe. There were, however, some notable exceptions. England, Switzerland, and the Scandinavian countries remained aloof. It followed, of course, that Roman Law did not become the groundwork of the political and constitutional system of the United States.

CHAPTER 16: *The Two Meanings of Law*

FROM what has already been said it will be realized how deep is the gulf which divides law in the sense in which it is defined by Justice Holmes—the American and British sense—from what has become known under the misleading title of Roman law. For Americans, Englishmen, Swiss, and Scandinavians, law is a social rule based on the willing consent of the citizens; it is *their* rule, which they have a share in framing, in interpreting (through judges in close touch with the mind of the community), and in enforcing. In Roman-law countries men do not look upon law in this way: for them it is a *command* imposed from above, from a tribunal or other seat of authority removed from the citizens and their way of life. By its perpetuation of the concept of law as a *command* the Roman Empire still maintains a stiffening (not to say deadening) influence over a large part of the political and social life of Europe, an influence which persisted even after the French Revolution and the adoption of democratic forms in France, Italy, and elsewhere in the nineteenth century.

CHAPTER 17: *The Ghost of the Roman Empire*

FORMALLY speaking, the Roman Empire came to an end in the West when in A.D. 476 the Senate voted that the Eastern Emperor in Constantinople should reign over the whole empire. Under this arrangement the government of Italy was entrusted to the chief of the German mercenaries previously in the service of the Western Empire. But the prestige of the Imperial City was too great to be thus summarily effaced. Rome lived on, not as a goverment, but as a repository of tradition, a model for imitation by later rulers. Some three centuries later one of these, Charles the Great, King of the Franks, crossed the Alps to receive the imperial crown and title at the hands of the Pope, becoming the founder of the Holy Roman Empire which was still surviving, though in shadowy form, in 1776.

43

Consider the effects of the Roman imperial tradition upon the political life of Europe. We will not dwell on the fact that it became a cause of perpetual rivalry and disorder during the Middle Age between the partisans of the revived empire and the papacy. What is important for these pages is that, when the medieval system eventually broke up, not through external conquest but through its own inner weakness, the local territorial rulers, who filled the vacuum of power, could not rid themselves of the imperial obsession. They saw themselves as emperors on a smaller scale and their kingdoms as portion of a world empire in the making; a curious illustration of this way of thinking occurred even in the present century, when the German Emperor, William II, styling himself "the Emperor of the Atlantic," designated the Czar of Russia as "the Emperor of the Pacific." And even the smaller states, to whom such hopes and dreams were denied, often followed the prevailing fashion of seeking aggrandizement, either by local adventures or as satellites of the great.

CHAPTER 18: *The Concept of Sovereignty*

THIS was the system—if system it can be called—which was prevailing in Europe when the people of the United States proclaimed their independence in 1776. It was one in which each state was bent on increasing its power and improving its position at the expense of its neighbors, near or far. It was, in fact, a system which was *competitive* through and through; only the rivalry was not a rivalry for wealth, as the name "competitive" suggests to our own minds today, but for power. The notion of co-operation, which was embodied in the medieval concept of a common Christendom, had receded completely into the background, even in the minds of thinkers.

These competing states were known as "sovereign" because, apart from a few exceptional cases, they were governed by in-

44

dividual sovereigns (*superani*), so called because they acknowledged no superiors whether within or without the borders of their dominions, or lordships. To their subjects, who belonged to a lower order of social existence, they were known by such titles as Emperor, King, Prince, or Grand Duke, distinctions roughly corresponding to the size of their territories and to the degree of their power. But in their relations with other sovereigns, the rulers of territories beyond the scope of their rule, they were all accounted equal. The prevailing rules of intercourse on the highest governmental level recognized no degrees of power between sovereigns.

In such circumstances, it would be natural for an outside observer to expect that, between the breakup of the medieval empire and the rise of the movement for a co-operative system on modern lines, Europe would have been in a state of chronic warfare. Wars of greater or smaller dimensions were indeed frequent during the four centuries, roughly between 1500 and 1914, when the concept of the sovereign state held undisputed sway. But the prevalence of what we should call today a state of "total warfare" was averted by three moderating influences.

CHAPTER 19: *The Balance of Power*

THE first of these moderating influences arose out of the nature of the power-political system itself. It was what would be called today a technical, almost a mechanical, device, carrying with it no philosophical implications, whether pessimistic or optimistic. It was the device known as the maintenance of the balance of power.

When a statesman sees that his territory is liable to be overwhelmed by a more powerful neighbor, what is more natural than that he should seek to counteract this danger by invoking the aid of another state sufficiently powerful to deter the possible aggressor? In the power vacuum following upon the European Middle Age recourse to this expedient became increasingly frequent; indeed, it was one of the factors which led sovereigns to keep representatives or envoys attached or accredited to the courts of their royal neighbors, thus bringing into existence the familiar diplomatic system of today.

In the working out of such plans of mutual aid, it was inevitable that the concept of supremacy or domination which, as we have seen, was theoretically inherent in the system, should become somewhat weakened in practice; for it could not be decently avowed as between allies and nominal equals. The issue which called for immediate attention was one of defense by means of mutual protection and the concept that fitted the situation was not that of imposing superior power but of measuring proportions of power or, as it came to be called, establishing a balance of power.

The concept of balance was admirably suited to the mentality of statesmen and diplomats in an age when politics and ethics had drawn wide apart. The scales of power knew nothing of moral values and could be skillfully adjusted to meet any situation. Thus, when considerations of the balance of power made it seem advisable to the sovereigns of Prussia, Austria, and Russia to diminish the territory of Poland and finally to wipe it off the map of Europe, this surgical operation, thrice renewed, with its accompanying distribution of the spoils, was carried out with a strict and almost pedantic adherence to the accepted rules of diplomatic practice. As this example reveals, the maintenance of the balance of power did not always exercise a moderating influence or prevent recourse to violence. But it did so increasingly as the years went on, particularly after the Napoleonic Wars, which caused such a shock to sovereigns everywhere and made them realize how hazardous an aggressive policy might be for their thrones. Thus in the nineteenth century, by force of habit, the balance of power became identified in European public opinion with the cause of peace and the two constantly figured together in official pronouncements by sovereigns and foreign ministers.

THE second moderating influence on the competition for power between sovereign states was provided by what was called "The Law of Nations" or, as it began to be called early in the nineteenth century, "International Law."

What is this international law, with which we shall be more and more closely concerned as we approch the problem of establishing world peace upon a firm basis?

International law, we are informed by its exponents, is the name given to the body of rules which are considered legally binding by civilized states in their dealings with one another.

To anyone who has followed the preceding argument it is clear at first sight that international law is not law in the Greek or American—not to say English or Swiss—sense of that important word. It grew up in the age of sovereignty, when the idea of basing power upon the consent of the people was unknown, or had died out, over the greater part of Europe. The fact that the word "law" has become attached to it is due to the survival in the minds of its exponents, and especially of the great Dutch writer Grotius, of the Stoic concept of natural law. Writing in an age of general European war, it seemed to Grotius that the competition between sovereigns for power, unrestrained by any limiting factor, was "unnatural," contrary to the nature of things, to the cosmic order, and to the nature of man himself. "There are some notions so certain," he wrote, "that no one can deny them without doing violence to his own nature." There *must* therefore, in the nature of things, be some limiting or restraining factor and to this Grotius, following the Stoic philosophers, gave the name of law; no doubt, he hoped that this august appellation would awaken some faint spark of awe or reverence in the minds of self-centered sovereigns.

We cannot pause to deal more fully with the concept of natural law, which is still a powerful intellectual and moral influence in

47

the world today. It is enough to say that, though it has caused much confusion in men's minds through the double sense of the word "law," it has rendered a positive service to civilization by providing a temporary bridge from the age of lawlessness to the age when constitutionalism upon a democratic basis began to acquire moral authority and political power in world affairs.

But, leaving aside the question of its name, it is impossible to deny that, in actual fact, international law, as it grew up and was employed in the age of sovereignty, was nothing more than the accepted etiquette, or body of customary rules of behavior, between sovereigns. To describe these rules as "legally binding" was simply a play upon words, for nothing was legally binding upon autocrats like Louis XIV or Frederick the Great. They followed the accepted rule when it suited them to do so. When it did not suit them, they employed an attorney, skilled in the rules, to find a good reason why they should ignore or contravene them. But, in the increasing complexity of intersovereign relations, it was certainly a convenience that such rules existed and had been collected into manuals of social behavior. To offend against conventional manners is to run a risk of incurring reprobation and thus furnishing a weapon to one's adversaries. To this extent international law constituted a restraining influence in the old diplomatic system.

CHAPTER 2 1: *British Sea Power*

WE come now to the third of the restraining influences referred to above, the influence of Britain and, in particular, of British sea power.

During the age of sovereignty Great Britain was never, in the full sense, part of the European political system. The cold-blooded mentality of its practitioners was foreign to her; and, though she often became deeply involved in Continental diplomacy, as in the coalition against Louis XIV and again against Napoleon, she

48

always took care to extricate herself as soon as she conveniently could. For the Roman influence had left England untouched and, though Englishmen did not always analyze to its depths the vital difference between their own cherished Common Law and what passed for law in the sovereign states of the Continent, they always felt in their bones that they represented a minority cause for which they might have to fight to the death at any time. Twice during the age of sovereignty events brought these apprehensions sharply to the surface—when in 1588 the Spanish monarch sent an Armada to destroy English sea power, and again in 1806 when the Emperor Napoleon assembled his ships at Boulogne to invade and crush his proudest and most persistent opponent.

From 1588 onward all Englishmen knew that their survival and that of their free institutions depended on their sea power; and, except for occasional vicissitudes, British power was predominant on the high seas from that year until toward the close of World War I.

Sea power and the balance of power fitted one another like a glove to the hand. Sea power, based on an island, is aloof from the political complications of the Continent and, like the scales of the balance, can be adjusted at any moment to a given situation. Moreover, it has the further advantage of being largely removed from the public view. While land armies, called in as a last remedy, carry through their cure acknowledged by visible tokens of recognition, the British Navy is known as "the silent service" and the treatment it has applied has very often been preventive rather than curative. No account of the age of sovereignty, and particularly of its last century, that between 1815 and 1914, would be complete without mention of the contribution made by British sea power to the sense of security which grew up on both sides of the Atlantic in the course of these generations. But, unfortunately for the scientific historian, the materials for such analysis are not easily gleaned from diplomatic archives.

Finally, a word about the British Navy, and what it represented in the mind of the British people, as a positive force—not merely as a force in the sense in which the practitioners of the balance of power understood force, but as an influence on the side of right against wrong. This comes out most clearly in the unceasing struggle for the suppression of the slave trade and the rescue of its unhappy victims; but it operated also in other fields of international action, as Continental statesmen were well aware. As a British naval historian proudly wrote a generation ago: "The White Ensign became the token of equal rights for all, a pledge of the brotherhood of all mankind."

1914

SECTION IV

1 9 1 4

For a century men have been laboring to solve
the Eastern Question. On the day when that
will be considered solved, Europe will find
itself confronted with the Austrian Question.

ALBERT SOREL, 1878

CHAPTER 22: *European Public Opinion in 1914*

THE outbreak of war in 1914 found Europeans with a divided
mind.

On the one hand they were shocked at the blow given by Germany and Austria-Hungary, acting together as allies, to what had
come to be known as "the public law of Europe," as represented
by the Concert of the Great Powers. This loose and incoherent
organization—if a body which had never even established a permanent secretariat can be described as an organization—had preserved Europe from a major conflict for nearly a hundred years
and had thus enabled a habit of peace and security to grow up in
men's minds. This was particularly the case in Great Britain,
which had never experienced large-scale war on her own soil and
where the Peace Movement had for generations been a powerful
undercurrent in public opinion. In the years immediately preceding
1914, the movement had been reinforced by a skillful presentation of the theme that war in a modern society, like that of the
twentieth century, would be injurious to all concerned and that

53

therefore for a power to resort to war would be foolish as well as wicked. The unintended effect of this reasoning upon the British mind was to divert its attention from the danger signals on the Continent. People who had become persuaded that war was outmoded all too easily went on to believe that it could not possibly take place—at least on a large scale; colonial wars, of course, were another matter.

Public opinion in Britain therefore, irrespective of party, expected the foreign secretary to use the time-honored instrument of the balance to prevent the outbreak of war, as had recently happened in the Balkans, or else to localize it, if it could not be entirely prevented. *Punch* was accurately interpreting the general sentiment when it pictured two old ladies exchanging their anxieties over the situation, one of them fearing the worst and the other reassuring her on the ground that "the Powers are sure to intervene." The idea that it was the Powers themselves who were now at loggerheads was slow to dawn on British minds.

Very different, on the other hand, was the state of opinion on the Continent. There the Peace Movement had never made more than a strictly limited appeal and in 1914 it was not merely counteracted by the traditions and methods of the Great Powers but also by a popular movement which had been gathering increasing momentum for a generation past—the movement of political nationalism.

Since this movement has been an important influence in keeping European and American opinion at cross-purposes, particularly since 1914, it cannot be omitted from a general survey of European political conditions, though it would be transgressing the limits of our subject to bring individual nations into the picture.

Political nationalism was an offspring of the French Revolution, which abolished the power of the sovereign monarch and replaced it by the power of the sovereign people.

Who or what was this sovereign people? This was a question which the French, with their critical minds, were soon asking and they answered it by introducing into the realm of practical politics a new and revolutionary concept—the concept of the *nation.*

54

In the United States the word "nation" is used, as a general term, to denote the whole body of citizens and carries with it no controversial associations. But in Continental Europe this is not so; for there the word has a cultural as well as a political context. For the European heirs of the French Revolution, a nation means a social group bound together primarily by a common sentiment. This sentiment, the sentiment of nationality, has been defined as one "of peculiar intimacy, intensity, and dignity, related to a definite home country." It will be realized at once how greatly this differs from the concept of citizenship. No doubt, citizenship is also a matter of sentiment, which is crystallized in the word "patriotism"; but, in the last analysis, it is a matter of law, of "papers." It is fixed by objective criteria. Nationality, on the other hand, is, in its very nature, subjective. A man is a Pole if he feels himself to be a Pole, whether he is a subject of Germany, Austria, or Russia.

When Frenchmen therefore began to think of themselves as members of a sovereign nation it was a great reinforcement to their natural pride; and so it was in the case of their European neighbors, near and far, who came under the spell of the new concept.

Nationalism, in this special European sense, had begun to spring up in the years preceding 1789 in other parts of the Continent, in countries as wide apart as Norway, Ireland, Italy, Greece, and Poland. But, whereas in France it was a movement which united and consolidated the French people by associating its powerful cultural tradition with its new regime of liberty, elsewhere on the Continent it often brought, not concord and union but strife and the sword. For few regions of Europe are as culturally homogeneous as France, and in nineteenth-century Europe the divergence between statehood and nationality became more pronounced as the movement spread from Western to Central and then to Eastern Europe.

In the middle of the century, in the climactic year 1848, the *political* demand for self-government and civic rights and the *national* demand for "a nation of our own" came to a head in a widespread popular outburst. As a result, the German national state and Italian national state were brought into existence by

1871. But at that point the movement was arrested. The imperial government at Vienna continued to bear sway over millions of "nationals" who were hoping and striving for the attainment of political freedom in a state of their own, with their own language, customs, and laws.

This movement had been gathering increasing momentum in the generation preceding 1914, and it was to this that the British Foreign Secretary referred when he told the Austro-Hungarian Ambassador in July, 1914, that, if war were to break out, all the issues of 1848 would be reawakened, with incalculable consequences for the life of Europe.

But hardly anyone in Britain had taken the trouble to think out the consequences which a return to 1848 would involve. This was a bottomless pit into which nobody dared to peer.

Moreover, few people realized—for their political leaders had not drawn attention to it—that Britain had a diplomatic link with the Continental system through her guarantee to Belgium, dating back to 1839.

Thus, when, in the last days of July and the first days of August, the war cloud, which had settled over Belgrade, moved suddenly to Brussels, the British people was taken entirely by surprise.

Mr. Winston Churchill has described World War II as "the unnecessary war." Looking back, one feels tempted to apply the same description to World War I. Had the German Emperor known for certain that Britain would honor her engagement to Belgium, it is a reasonable inference from his ambivalent state of mind, as revealed by the documents, that he would have urged caution on the Austro-Hungarian emissary who visited Berlin after the murder of the Archduke, instead of giving him the green light.

But why, one asks, did the Emperor so completely misjudge the reaction of British opinion to the invasion of Belgium? It was because those responsible for British policy had not previously kept the British people sufficiently informed as to the explosive character of the European situation and its bearings upon Britain herself.

Had the crisis of July, 1914, passed off without a general war, would not the danger have been certain to recur at an early date— for instance, on the death of the Emperor Francis Joseph? No doubt; but, in that event, statesmen, including American statesmen, would have been more ready for it and the commotion resulting from the breakup of the Austro-Hungarian Empire might well have been localized, like the commotion caused only a few years earlier at the breakup of the old Turkish Empire in the Balkans.

In contrast with the state of things in Britain, public opinion on the Continent, from the shores of the Channel and the North Sea to those of the Baltic and the Aegean, was much better prepared for the drama that was about to be unfolded. This can perhaps best be illustrated by a personal incident. When, in the summer of 1910, the writer visited the island of Crete and climbed Mount Ida, he went into a shepherd's hut not far from the summit, some 8,000 feet above the sea, and asked for a glass of milk. In the ensuing conversation the Greek shepherd wanted to know his opinion on what would happen in Southeastern Europe on the death of the Emperor Francis Joseph. That lonely shepherd, high above daily newspapers and the clamor of propaganda, was thinking in terms of 1848, as were millions of others in all the lands east of Vienna.

CHAPTER 23: *The War as it Appeared to Europeans*

THE war which ensued, as we can now view it in perspective after nearly two generations, may be entitled the first or purely European phase of World War I.

Seen as the outcome of the conditions described in the preceding pages, it was an explosion of forces which had been gathering under the surface of European life since 1848 or, in some cases, even further back, since the French Revolution.

The American Road to World Peace

In this general melee, in which nations as well as states became involved, four particular contests can be distinguished. There was first a contest between the Russian Empire of the Czars and the Austro-Hungarian Monarchy of the Hapsburgs, the issue at stake being predominance in Eastern Europe. There was, secondly, a contest between France and Britain on the one hand and Imperial Germany on the other, the issue at stake being predominance in Western Europe. There was, thirdly, a contest between Germany and Great Britain, the issue at stake being British sea power; and finally, coming to a head a year later, in 1915, there was a contest between Austria-Hungary and Italy, the stake being certain Italian-speaking lands in the Eastern Alps and along the coast of the Adriatic Sea.

In military terms, these contests between states became rolled together into one, a contest between two combinations of European Great Powers—one known as an Alliance and the other as an Entente—the former comprising Germany and Austria-Hungary and the latter Great Britain, France, Russia, and Italy. But it must be remembered that in the armies of Austria-Hungary and Russia there were large numbers of individual fighting men—Poles, Czecho-Slovaks, and others—whose hearts were in a different cause.

By 1917 the two groups had become virtually deadlocked and Americans awoke to the fact that the security of the smaller World Island was involved in the struggle that was going on in the larger and on the surrounding oceans. But before matters reached this point, nearly three years had passed, during which the American people was becoming accustomed to see Europe, hitherto its senior partner in world affairs, in a new light and to realize the extent to which the endangering of the cause of freedom in the larger World Island involved a threat to the smaller.

Thus Europe and America, two separate political worlds, with the British-dominated ocean between them and preventing the one from impinging on the other, were brought sharply into confrontation—Europe, where power had for two thousand years been the ruling political concept, and America, the hopeful and forward-looking upholder of freedom.

WOODROW WILSON AND ELIHU ROOT

SECTION V

WOODROW WILSON AND
ELIHU ROOT

"In foreign affairs we have been guided by principles clearly conceived, and consistently lived up to. Perhaps they have not been fully comprehended because they have hitherto governed international affairs only in theory, but not in practice."

> WOODROW WILSON:
> *Acceptance speech on*
> *renomination, September 2, 1916*

"An international breach of the peace is a matter which concerns every member of the Community of Nations."

> ELIHU ROOT:
> *Letter to Colonel House,*
> *August 16, 1918*

CHAPTER 24: *Why Woodrow Wilson was*
Not Understood

WHEN the European War, as men were to go on calling it for another three years, broke out in August, 1914, European statesmen must have realized that the old European diplomatic system had received a blow from which it might never recover. But none of them could perceive what might take its place—not even the most levelheaded and thoughtful amongst them, the British Foreign Secretary, Sir Edward Grey. None of them could see beyond the narrow limits of the system of sovereign states which they had inherited from their predecessors and in which they had been trained to work. When they tried to fix their minds on a constructive policy to prevent another similar disaster in the future, they found that they were intellectually bankrupt: they and their advisers could only suggest fresh combinations and permutations of old eighteenth and nineteenth century devices, new treaties and guarantees, new pledges given by sovereign states to other sovereign states. Thus when the words "League of Nations" fell upon their tired ears, though they were ready to listen, and though the President of the United States spoke to them in language recalling their own masterpieces of eloquence, they could not understand what he was trying to tell them. His simple words did not seem to make sense.

There were three good reasons why Woodrow Wilson's ideas did not register in the minds of European statesmen and their experts.

The first was that Woodrow Wilson spoke as an exponent of American ideas. But few people in Europe at that time understood America and, with the exception of James Bryce, these were not in touch with the chancelleries. So they were inclined to write off the President's references to American principles as mere idealistic verbiage framed for an emotional democratic public and to look for something more solid concealed behind it; and that solid substance they failed to find.

The second reason why the President's words did not register was because he was a political scientist, while most of the European statesmen and their advisers had been trained in the law. To Woodrow Wilson the problem posed by the breakdown of the European system, apart from the moral aspect, which, of course bulked largely in his mind, was political in the narrow sense. Its solution called for the exercise of political technique—technique of the kind possessed by the Fathers of the American Constitution

and the authors of *The Federalist*. But this was unfamiliar ground
for the inmates of the European Foreign Offices. So, in this respect
also, the two sets of minds did not meet.

The third reason was that Woodrow Wilson never set forth
his own ideas in detail; indeed, he very carefully avoided doing
so. One can piece them together in retrospect from his public
addresses and from the reminiscences of those who talked with
him, in particular, from Colonel House. But there is no connected
record, such as one could have expected from so methodical a
thinker. One suspects that the reason why he was always so reluctant to do this was because he knew that to carry his thinking
further in public would be to arouse a storm of opposition, an
opposition coming, not only from European statesmen and intellectuals, but from similar quarters in his own country; he was
aware that, apart from exceptional cases, like that of Elihu Root,
who was much more than a lawyer, he would have the great bulk
of the lawyers, especially the international lawyers, against him.

Under these circumstances, Woodrow Wilson may well have
felt that it would be better not to put forward a definite clear-cut
plan as a substitute for the old European system which had broken
down. Rather, he would suggest the *direction* in which statesmen
might move *toward* a new order and make a tentative beginning
on what he, as a political scientist, considered were the right
lines.

This shrewd and patient policy proved successful. Though
neither the League of Nations Covenant nor its successor, the
United Nations Charter, are full-fledged constitutional documents, they are incontestably experiments in political construction, and, as such, in the true line of succession from the framers
of the United States Constitution. That Woodrow Wilson persuaded the European statesmen to accept the Covenant was a victory the full nature of which was not understood at that time and
is only now beginning to be appreciated in retrospect. For the
world is now committed to the American approach—which is a
political science approach—to the problem of world order.

CHAPTER 25: *The Larger Design*

LET us suppose that Woodrow Wilson, with his broad knowledge of the past, had opened his whole mind to the listening peoples. What might he have told them?

He might have said that political development in the Old World had come to a dead end because it was blocked by the concept of sovereignty, which prevented Europeans from regarding one another as friends and neighbors. Europe, he might have gone on to explain, had missed a great opportunity at the time of the French Revolution. That was the moment when she was free to make a clean break with her past habits and to switch her political progress on to new and more forward-looking lines. As the movement for national liberation and self-government, originating in France, spread from country to country, the European peoples might have caught the spirit of free America and devised their new democratic institutions in terms of political and social co-operation rather than of competition for power. That would have been the true interpretation of the three great watchwords of the French Revolution: Liberty, Equality, Fraternity.

Had that taken place in those years, Europe would by 1914 have been transformed from a group of separate and self-centered nations, each bent on increasing its own importance and prestige, into a *community* inspired by the vitality and *élan* of the New World. Each nation would have preserved, and would have indeed developed more fully, its own characteristic genius, but together they would have given the ancient Continent, with its Christian and classical background, a new mind and an enriched soul.

Thus the Old World and the New might have marched together into the future. And since, as the French say, it is never too late to do the right thing (*il n'est jamais tard pour bien faire*), they could still march together today—so Woodrow Wilson might

64

have continued his appeal—if the European peoples and their leaders, taught by common suffering, would cast away the false interpretations of the great revolutionary watchwords— interpretations which they had been misled by false guides into adopting in the nineteenth century.

From that point he might have gone on to develop the theme of community and to show how, under a system of government of the people, for the people, by the people, all sorts and conditions of mankind can be enabled to live and prosper harmoniously together in a free society. Under such a system all men feel at home and take a natural pride in their government and institutions. But that does not make them feel unfriendly or suspicious toward their neighbors, as the unfortified frontier with Canada bears eloquent witness. There is no reason in the nature of things, he could have said, why the pattern of United States-Canadian relations should not be extended the world over, till the whole earth becomes a single community of political friends and neighbors.

This was not an idle fancy, a mere daydream, he might have told them, for it had already taken place in miniature on the soil of war-scarred Europe. The Swiss Confederation, the best governed state in the world, is an organic union of local communities which, starting with an agreement between the inhabitants of three mountain valleys, has grown until it embraces the greater part of the Alpine region of Europe. The Swiss, who have discovered how to harmonize four cultures within a single political community, are the only people in Europe fully capable of understanding the United States; but they cannot explain the United States to their fellow Europeans because so few Europeans outside Switzerland understand the nature and spirit of Swiss institutions, familiar though a great many of them are with these in books, because the general political life of Europe has developed on quite different lines.

That Woodrow Wilson had some such thoughts one may guess from his conference on shipboard on the way to Europe in December, 1918, as recorded by Isaiah Bowman. But he refrained from giving vent to them. And in this, no doubt, he was wise; for there were at the time only two leading thinkers in Europe of whom we can be quite certain that they would have understood Woodrow Wilson's thought: Thomas G. Masaryk, the sage of Czecho-Slovakia, and Max Huber, the sage of Switzerland.

CHAPTER 26: *The Dilemma of the World Authority*

THUS Woodrow Wilson never formulated what we may call *the dilemma of the world authority*—a kindred dilemma to that already set forth on the subject of democracy.

The dilemma is as follows:

1. The interdependence of public affairs in the present-day world renders some form of world authority necessary in the interest of civilization.

2. Such a world authority must rest on a basis of popular consent, so as to safeguard the world against tyranny.

3. This calls for some sort of *political community* to provide such consent.

4. Such a community does not exist as yet in Europe—much less in the rest of the World Island.

5. How then can a world authority be brought into existence?

CHAPTER 27: *Peace and Liberty*

LET us now look at the issues facing Woodrow Wilson from the point of view of our specific problem—the establishment of some sort of world authority.

66

Woodrow Wilson and Elihu Root

When the American people, in August, 1914, saw all Europe ablaze from East to West, their first reaction was one of astonishment and horror. It seemed to them impossible that such events should take place in the twentieth century, even on the larger and wickeder world island. In this respect their reaction resembled that of the British, but they enjoyed the immeasurable advantage of not being linked to the European diplomatic system by a treaty obligation. They were therefore free to consider the changed world situation at leisure.

President Wilson was at one with the great majority of the American people in sharing this detached attitude; indeed, he took the lead in promoting it. He was all the more able to do so because, as a historian and political scientist, he understood the nature of the forces which were now in eruption and could bring a scholarly judgment to bear upon the conflict as it developed. When, in speaking of the war, he told the American people, on May 27, 1916, as the period of neutrality was drawing to its close, that they were "not concerned with its causes and objects" nor in discovering "the obscure fountains from which its stupendous flood" had "burst forth," these words did not mean, as they were taken to mean in some European quarters, that he dismissed the causes of the war as unimportant or that he refused to pass a moral judgment upon them. On the contrary, as his whole action after April, 1917, showed, he regarded them as highly important, both in themselves and in their bearings on the United States. But what was principally in his mind at that time was, as he said in his neutrality proclamation of August 19, 1914, that "the people of the United States" were "drawn from many nations and particularly from the nations now at war."

Thus, though he felt it incumbent on him, as chief magistrate of the nation, to enjoin the duty of "impartiality" as opposed to "partisanship" with this or that of the contending European nations, he did so, not as an unconcerned spectator, but with a definite set of principles in his mind which he was doing his best to put into practice as far as circumstances made it possible. Some of these took the form of what may be called "short-distance policies," promulgated during the period of neutrality; others, more deeply

67

conceived, only came to fruition after the United States had joined the ranks of the nations engaged in vindicating the cause of freedom. But it is important to remember the inner connection between them, which was not apparent to all in the heat of controversy at the time; for they were all in their own way characteristically American policies.

The President's short-distance policies were set forth, as was appropriate, in his second annual message to Congress, delivered on December 8, 1914. The greater part of the message was devoted to domestic affairs, but, before he closed, he added a "few words" about the subject which was in everyone's mind, "upon which," as he said, "it is highly important that our judgments should be clear, definite, and steadfast."

He did not discuss the European situation itself, but confined himself to urging the need, at such a time, for an adequate system of national defense. This should "include, in the first place, a powerful navy, the dimensions of which," and their relation to the navies of other Powers, he left unspecified: and it should include, in the second place, a system of national military training "by which every citizen who will volunteer may be made familiar with the use of modern arms, the rudiments of drill and maneuver and the maintenance and sanitation of camps." Such arrangements, he considered, would be sufficient at a time when the United States was "at peace with all the world" and when there was "no reason to fear that from any quarter our independence or the integrity of our territory is threatened."

Let us note in passing, as we shall be returning to this subject, that, in thus encouraging citizens to undergo military training on these lines, President Wilson was endorsing what may be called the Swiss philosophy on the matter of the place of armaments in a democracy, the philosophy which, as contrasted with "militarism" on the one hand and "pacifism" on the other, regards military service as a part of the duty of the responsible citizen in a free country.

But the President took occasion, in his message to the Congress, to introduce a further thought. In a brief passage, in which he did not enter into particulars, he expressed his hope and that of the

American people, that their "character and reputation" might "presently, in God's providence, bring" them "an opportunity such as has seldom been vouchsafed any nation, the opportunity to counsel and obtain peace in the world and reconciliation and a healing settlement of many a matter which has cooled and interrupted the friendship of nations." "This," he continued, "is the time above others when we should wish and resolve to keep our strength by self-possession, our influence by preserving our ancient principles of action."

This is the question which Woodrow Wilson, who always felt himself to be an educator as well as a statesman, threw open to the American people for their consideration in this first phase of his teaching on world affairs. It is a question which it took them some thirty years to discuss and to think out before they found the answer.

CHAPTER 28: *Woodrow Wilson and the Hague Conference System*

THE President's words cited in the preceeding chapter, reveal his expectation that, at the close of hostilities, there would be an international conference, in which the United States would take part, and that this conference would bring an "opportunity" to "obtain peace in the world." But what kind of peace? A peace on *American* lines and applying American "principles of action." That is the thought between the lines of this carefully prepared message, as we can see in the light of after-events.

Now, in using such language the President was passing over in silence another set of principles, espoused by many leading Americans at that time, which carried a label marked, not "American," but "international." This set of principles bore a judicial hallmark and was associated with the two peace conferences which had taken place at The Hague in 1899 and 1907. The President spoke, not on this occasion only but throughout his public references to peace and the League of Nations, as though the Hague Conferences had never taken place.

His attitude on the subject was brought out most clearly in a speech delivered on February 1, 1916, at Des Moines, Iowa. "What is America expected to do?" he asked his Middle Western audience. "She is expected to do nothing less than to keep law alive while the rest of the world burns. You know there is no international tribunal, my fellow citizens. I pray God that, if this contest has no other result, it will at least have the result of creating an international tribunal and producing some sort of guarantee of peace on the part of the great nations of the world. But it has not yet done that, and the only thing that keeps America out of danger is that, to some degree, the understandings, the ancient and honorable understanding of nations with regard to their relations to one another and to the citizens of one another, are to some extent still observed and followed. And wherever there is a departure from them, the United States is called upon to intervene, to speak the voice of protest, to speak the voice of insistence."

No one hearing or reading these words, unless he was a specialist in the subject, would have guessed that there was actually in existence at that time an international tribunal—the Permanent Court of Arbitration, set up by the First Hague Conference of 1899. This was indeed not a court in the usual sense of the term, since it had no set of judges. But it had all the framework needed for a court—a body of rules, a list of suitable arbitrators available for the choice of the parties, and a permanent secretariat.

But Woodrow Wilson used even clearer language on this subject in an address delivered in the very Mecca of the lawyers, the International Law Society in Paris, on May 9, 1919. "International law," he told them, "has perhaps sometimes been a little too much thought out in the closet. International law has—may I say it without offense?—been handled too exclusively by lawyers. Lawyers like definite lines. They like systematic arrangements. They are uneasy if they depart from what was done yesterday. They dread experiments. They like charted seas, and if they have no charts, hardly venture to undertake the voyage. Now we must venture upon uncharted seas, to some extent, in the future. In the New League of Nations we are starting out on uncharted seas and therefore we must have, I will not say the audacity, but the steadiness of purpose which is necessary in such novel circumstances."

Why did Woodrow Wilson thus speak as though the Hague Conference institution did not exist? It was because the events of July, 1914, had taught him the lesson, which some other eminent persons, on both sides of the Atlantic, were slow to learn, that the European War had not broken out owing to the absence of preventive machinery. It broke out because the aggressors refused to avail themselves of machinery which actually existed. Why did they take up this attitude? Because true to the power-political tradition, they *lacked the will to co-operate*. Why were they not forced to do so, or at least to refrain from resorting to violence? Because they were *Great Powers*. Had they been small and weak, the great would have found a way of dealing with them. But who could coerce the Great Powers? To the European statesmen of that day, that would have seemed like interfering with a law of nature—or, in the words of Woodrow Wilson, venturing on an uncharted sea.

The events of July and August, 1914, in which the authority of the Hague Conference was swept away like a house of cards, made a lasting impression on Woodrow Wilson's mind. He realized, as the more legalistically minded were reluctant to do, that the work of the Hague could not be taken up afresh until it could be underpinned by a firm foundation of morality, of what he called "ancient and honorable understandings." He saw no future for the body of rules known as "international law" unless it was part of a larger system, a system of a community of nations acknowledging common ethical principles and inspired by the mutual confidence springing from such principles.

Woodrow Wilson knew that such confidence could not be created simply by the setting up of new legal machinery, however great an improvement on what preceded it. That was why his mind turned away from The Hague and why matters covering the ground of the Hague treaties were entrusted in the Covenant to a political body, the Council of the League of Nations.

CHAPTER 29: *Open Covenants*

IN his address to Congress on January 9, 1918, so anxiously awaited in Europe, Woodrow Wilson placed at the head of his Fourteen Points, outlining "the program of the world's peace . . . the only possible program as we see it," the following conditions:

"Open covenants of peace, openly arrived at, after which there shall be no private international understandings of any kind, but diplomacy shall always proceed frankly and in the public view."

These words caused a profound stir in the chancelleries; for the proposal was quite unexpected and at first sight it seemed impracticable and dangerous. Experienced diplomats argued that it could not possibly be carried out and that to try to do so would be to open up all kinds of new sources of trouble.

But Woodrow Wilson knew what he was doing when he put "Open Covenants" at the head of his list; for it was the clearest illustration of the difference between the old diplomatic system and the new methods of which the League of Nations was to be the vehicle. Of course, what he was advocating would be a breach with diplomatic precedent. Europe had grown used to the black-coated emissary from the New World. She would get used to the new methods of diplomacy necessitated by the new conditions— and the sooner the better. Hence the placing of the subject at the head of the list. After well-nigh two generations, we are so used to "diplomacy proceeding" more and more "in the public view" that we have almost forgotten what the conditions were which Woodrow Wilson set himself to redress.

Woodrow Wilson and Elihu Root

Foreign policy was the last redoubt of old-fashioned power, the last fastness which held out against control by the people. In three of the six European Great Powers of 1914,—Germany, Austria-Hungary, and Russia,—foreign affairs were wholly in the hands of the monarch, or of a foreign minister responsible exclusively to him. In France and Italy there was a semblance of parliamentary control: but as these governments were empowered to commit the parliaments and peoples to treaty engagements the terms of which, for obvious security motives, were kept secret, there could be no adequate popular discussion, still less popular control, in the absence of adequate information. In Britain the conditions were somewhat different, as the British people had been for centuries on the alert as to any happenings abroad in which they might be involved. But the possession of supreme sea power made it seem less necessary for the foreign minister to take them into his confidence on matters of lesser importance. All through Queen Victoria's reign, the sovereign had still a considerable say on the conduct of foreign policy. As late as the eighteen eighties Lord Salisbury entered into a secret treaty with Italy without informing the British people and the House of Commons. When his successor, Lord Rosebery, assumed his office and was told of the document by the permanent undersecretary, he refused to take cognizance of it and so one more harmful custom died out. But not without regrets on the part of the experts, who argued that, if one was in the game at all, one ought to play it according to the existing rules. Under those rules, the conduct of foreign relations was carried on, under the seal of confidence, as between gentlemen of honor. If one of the parties insisted on disclosing these "secrets" to the people, and thus to all the world, the result would be that he would forfeit the advantage of being entrusted with precious information, which might be of vital importance to the national security.

Thus secret diplomacy was inextricably bound up with the whole European system, with its atmosphere of mutual suspicion and its plotting and counterplotting. In Woodrow Wilson's eyes all this should be, and could be, swept away once and for all, and in the new atmosphere of the League of Nations, where the spirit of mutual co-operation, natural to Americans, would be dominant,

73

appropriate new methods would be devised. One of them, laid down in Article 18 of the Covenant, would be the registration of all international treaties and engagements, which would not be binding unless they had been so dealt with.

How could Woodrow Wilson be expected to foresee that Article 18 would be brought into force, and the diplomats assembled at Geneva would work out the required new procedures, without the restraining presence, the co-operation, and experience of those who suggested the new approach?

CHAPTER 30:   *The Freedom of the Seas and Freedom of Trade*

THE reason why peace and liberty were so difficult to reconcile was because the ancient principles no longer fitted the new situation which the American people had to face in 1914.

What were those principles? They were the principles outlined in the preceding pages, which *took for granted* the existence of a friendly world, in which men and nations were willing and ready to co-operate in their mutual dealings, whether at home or abroad.

It was this co-operation which, in the President's formulation of policy between 1914 and 1917, found expression in the principle of "the freedom of the seas"—a freedom closely related in his mind to freedom in the domestic sphere. For, on the high seas, friendly co-operation had, during the nineteenth century—that is, almost from the earliest days of the republic—become not simply a habit but one might say a *climate*. During those generations, when free trade was the accepted economic policy, not only in Great Britain but in Europe, international intercourse had multiplied a thousandfold, until what had been rare luxuries in the eighteenth century had become household articles in the life of the ordinary citizen. The immense improvement in the standard of life of the Western peoples which had resulted from this was not primarily due, as has sometimes been claimed, to the so-called "capitalist system"—capital is an instrument which tyrants in all ages from the Pharaohs onward have known how to turn to their own uses— but to the spirit of enterprise which animated merchants and manufacturers and to the nature of the political system which facilitated their activities. But, above all, this world-wide "mercantile republic," as Adam Smith called it, owed its growth and maintenance to the fact that it was shielded by British sea power.

In time of peace the British Navy protected merchant ships, whatever flag they might fly, in the pursuance of their business or, in the time-honored British phrase, of their "lawful occasions." But, when Britain herself was involved in hostilities, these peace-keeping functions changed their character and became a formidable instrument of war, which might interfere with the commerce of the United States and even involve a threat to its political interests. This danger, which might have become serious, had the Germans pursued a less reckless policy, was removed when the United States entered the war and the two navies joined together against the common enemy. But that it still remained in the President's mind was clear from the fact that, as late as January, 1918, the second in order of his Fourteen Points stipulated, as part of "the only possible program of the world's peace," "absolute freedom of navigation upon the seas, outside territorial waters, alike in peace and in war, except as the seas may be closed in whole or in part by international action for the enforcement of international covenants."

In the same order of thinking we may place the Third Point, stipulating for "the removal so far as possible, of all economic barriers and the establishment of an equality of trade conditions among all nations consenting to the peace and associating themselves for its maintenance." On this it is enough to say, at this point, that sound though this doctrine is, both from a nineteenth-century and from a twentieth-century point of view, it was not found possible in 1919, and has not yet been found possible in 1952, to implement it in the form of an International Trade Organization.

CHAPTER 31: *The League of Nations*

THE entry of the United States into the war in April, 1917, on the side of the forces of freedom brought about no change in the political philosophy and principles of Woodrow Wilson, which, as he had said in his renomination speech some months earlier, were "clearly conceived." But it did bring about an important change in his *attitude*. He no longer thought and felt as an *outsider*. He had become an insider; and the concept which more and more dominated his thinking was that of *community*.

As we saw in the preceding pages, community is a concept which is at the very heart of American life. It is a concept which takes a "friendly world" for granted—a *social* concept, providing a basis on which political problems can be worked out in an atmosphere of mutual confidence.

When Woodrow Wilson became an "insider," his natural inclination was to view this "inside," his new environment, through American eyes, to seek out what elements there were in the old European system which could be used to turn it into a true community and to build upon them. This is the central idea of the League of Nations.

He had already given expression to this thought on January 22, 1917, before the final break with Germany, but when events were fast moving in that direction. "The question," he told the Senate, "upon which the whole future peace and policy of the world depends is this: Is the present war a struggle for a just and secure peace, or only for a new balance of power? If it be only a struggle for a new balance of power," he asked,—and the question is still pertinent today,—"who will guarantee, who can guarantee the stable equilibrium of the new arrangement? . . . There must be, not a balance of power, but a *community of power*, not organized rivalries, but an *organized common peace*." Two and a half months later he carried his thought a stage further forward, flinging a

76

challenge at Machiavelli and at the whole Continental European diplomatic tradition: "We are," he told the Congress, "at the beginning of an age in which it will be insisted that the same standard of responsibility for wrong done shall be observed among nations and their governments that are observed among the individual citizens of civilized states. A steadfast concert for peace can never be maintained except by a partnership of democratic nations. No autocratic government could be trusted to keep faith within it or observe its covenants. It must be a league of honor, a partnership of opinion. Intrigue would eat its vitals away; the plottings of inner circles who could plan what they would and render account to no one would be a corruption seated at its very heart. Only free peoples can hold their purpose and their honor steady to a common end and prefer the interests of mankind to any narrow interest of their own."

In thus crystallizing the idea of community the President had been able to profit by the latest thinking of the most eminent American jurist of the day and the outstanding member of the Republican party, Senator Elihu Root. Here is Senator Root's letter for communication to the President through Colonel House—a letter which is one of the classics of American political writing.

Clinton, New York
August 16, 1918

My dear Colonel House:

I promised to give you in writing the substance of some things I said during the luncheon at your apartment sometime ago:

The first requisite for any durable concert of peaceable nations to prevent war is a fundamental change in the principle to be applied to international breaches of the peace.

The view now assumed and generally applied is that the use of force by one nation toward another is a matter in which only the two nations concerned are primarily interested, and if any other nation claims a right to be heard on the subject it must show some specific interest of its own in the controversy. That burden of proof rests upon any other nation which seeks to take part if it will relieve itself of the charge of impertinent interference and avoid the resentment which always meets impertinent interference in the affairs of an independent sovereign state. This view was illustrated by Germany in July, 1914, when she insisted that the invasion of Serbia by Austria-Hungary was a matter which solely concerned two states, and upon substantially that ground refused to agree to the conference proposed by Sir Edward Grey. The requisite change is an abandonment of this view and a universal, formal and irrevocable acceptance of the view that an international breach of the peace is a matter which concerns every member of the Community of Nations—a matter in which every nation has a direct interest and to which every nation has a right to object.

These two views correspond to the two kinds of responsibility in municipal law which we call civil responsibility and criminal responsibility. If I make a contract with you and break it, it is no business of our neighbor. You can sue me or submit, and he has nothing to say about it. On the other hand, if I assault and batter you, every neighbor has an interest in having me arrested and punished, because his own safety requires that violence shall be restrained. At the basis of every community lies the idea of organization to preserve the peace. Without that idea really active and controlling there can be no community of individuals or of nations. It is the gradual growth and substitution of this idea of community interest in preventing and punishing breaches of the peace which has done away with private war among civilized peoples.

The Monroe Doctrine asserted a specific interest on the part of the United States in preventing certain gross breaches of the peace on the American Continent; and when President Wilson suggested an enlargement of the Monroe Doctrine to take in the whole world, his proposal carried by necessary implications the change of doctrine which I am discussing. The change may seem so natural as to be unimportant, but it is really crucial, for the old doctrine is asserted and the broader doctrine is denied by approximately half the military power of the world, and the question between the two is one of the things about which the war is being fought. The change involves a limitation of sovereignty, making every sovereign state subject to the superior right of a community of sovereign states to have the peace preserved. The acceptance of any such principle would be fatal to the whole Prussian theory of the state and of government. When you have got this principle accepted openly, expressly, distinctly, un-equivocally by the whole civilized world, you will for the first time have a Community of Nations, and the practical results which will naturally develop will be as different from those which have come from the old view of national responsibility as are the results which flow from the American Declaration of In-dependence compared with the results which flow from the Divine Right of Kings.

Thirty-four years after these words were written, there are still too many on both sides of the Atlantic who refuse to grasp the importance of this "crucial" difference.

It is not necessary to recount here how the Covenant of the League of Nations was drafted or to analyze its provisions. Seen in perspective, two elements stand out as all-important. One is that which is so well brought out in the Root letter—the "fundamental change" in political thinking in regard to war, or, as Root preferred to say "international breaches of the peace." To commit a breach of the peace henceforward would become a *crime*. This is not stated in so many words in the Covenant, for it was at that time still too strong meat for the European chancelleries. But it is the clear underlying sense of Article XI of the Covenant, the Article which was drawn up on the inspiration of Senator Root's letter. The first sentence of that Article runs as follows: "Any war or threat of war, whether immediately affecting any of the members of the League or not, is hereby declared a matter of concern to the whole League, and the League shall take any action that may be deemed wise and effectual to safeguard the peace of nations." As we shall see, the substance of this article was later embodied in the United Nations Charter.

The other outstanding element in the Covenant was that it set up an *institution*, or rather a whole set of interlocking institutions. This was something entirely novel on the highest level of diplo-matic action. As we have already remarked, the Concert of the Great Powers possessed no permanent organization, not even a secretariat. True to their self-regarding traditions, the Great Powers did business together, when ambassadors did not suffice, by means of conferences, each one of which was organized separately; and this improvised organization was dismantled at the close of the proceedings. What the Covenant did was to take the individual foreign ministers and diplomats and to make them members of a continuing community, the "Council" and "Assembly" of the League of Nations.

We have become so used to those international gatherings that we have forgotten what an innovation they were in the days when the concept of sovereignty, that is to say, of self-centered power, still held sway in the chancelleries of Europe. For a foreign minister to know that, in so many weeks' time, he will be facing his opposite number in another country and must be ready to answer his points in public debate or in private conversation involves a most salutary discipline—a discipline in *social behavior*. If the League of Nations had done no more than that, it would already have rendered most valuable service.

CHAPTER 32: *The Reduction of Armaments*

THE Covenant of the League of Nations consists of 26 Articles. The first seven of these deal with the internal organization of the League of Nations. In the leading place, as the first Article concerned with matters of substance, stands Article 8 dealing with the reduction of armaments. The first two paragraphs of this famous (or notorious) Article run as follows:

> The Members of the League recognize that the maintenance of peace requires the reduction of national armaments to the lowest point consistent with national safety and the enforcement by common action of international obligations.
> The Council, taking account of the geographical situation and circumstances of each State, shall formulate plans for such reduction for the consideration and action of the several governments.

80

Thus the first paragraph of the Article lays down a philosophy and the second a procedure.

The important word in the first paragraph is "requires." Peace, it says, in effect, cannot be maintained unless armaments are reduced, or, in telegraphic language: "armaments mean war." This is, of course, just not so. The notion that armaments mean war is a popular mistake, amply contradicted by history. But it is a very widespread and deep-rooted mistake, a favorite theme in pulpits as well as on platforms, and a mistake which, if allowed to pass uncontradicted, can do infinite damage to the cause of peace. Woodrow Wilson was not a victim of this mistake. As we have already seen, he regarded armaments as a necessary instrument in the carrying out of a sound international policy or, in his own words, in "the enforcement of international covenants." According to this philosophy, the aim should be, not to *abolish* armaments but to make them *instruments of international co-operation*. Once governments have learned to look upon them in that light, competition in armaments will cease and their reduction will follow automatically. Co-operative armament will not only maintain peace, but it will also lighten the burden of taxation. It will be both cheap and effective.

We may put the same thought in another way. Armaments are not a cause of international tension; they are a *symptom*, a barometer, and barometers do not cause storms. The *cause* of international tension is the unneighborly spirit of the powers concerned and their unwillingness to discuss their differences in a reasonable spirit. Thus to imagine that the reduction of armaments would, of itself, lead to an improvement in international relations is to put the cart before the horse. When an unreasonable temper prevails among the parties to a disarmament conference, discussion does not allay trouble; it *makes* trouble. So far from smoothing away existing difficulties, it exacerbates them and opens up new sources of controversy. What could be better calculated to make bad blood than to ask a group of jealous, self-important, and mutually suspicious sovereign states to agree on a *scale* of armaments from which they are to pledge themselves not to depart?

Thus, if we may anticipate already at this stage of our inquiry

81

the consequences of the insertion of armaments reduction into
the Covenant as an *obligation* assumed by the members of the
League of Nations, we can sum them up in a few words. The long-
drawn discussions, which began in the First Assembly in 1920
with the setting up of the Temporary Mixed Commission for the
Reduction of Armaments and finally petered out in 1934, failed
completely to produce the "plans" which the Council of the
League was bound by Article 8 of the Covenant to "formulate";
but they did result in undermining the morale of the French people
and in supplying the Hitler regime, in the form of the slogan
"equality of armament," with a powerful instrument for destroying the Treaty of Versailles and thus paving the way for World
War II.

For this ill-starred chain of events the United States government
was only responsible in a minor degree and Woodrow Wilson, as
the chief architect of the League of Nations, can hardly be held
responsible at all; for the practical decisions which launched the
League on this policy in 1920 were taken after the United States
had retired from the European scene.

But it is time to return to Woodrow Wilson.

That it would have been better if the question of armaments
had not been raised at all we may agree in the light of after-events.
But "disarmament" and the "Peace Movement" had for so long
been associated together in the American mind that it would have
been difficult for the President to submit the subject to the "silent
treatment" which he meted out to the Hague Conference system.
As it was, he approached it with extreme prudence. Point 4 of the
Fourteen Points, in which he formulated his policy on the subject,
opens with the words "adequate guarantees"—those guarantees
which the United States is still seeking in the Atomic Age. The
wording of the Point is as follows:

> Adequate guarantees given and taken that national armaments
> will be reduced to the lowest points consistent with domestic
> safety.

Later, but before the draft was presented to the Peace Conference, the President added a concluding clause: "And the enforce-

ment by common action of international obligations." There is no trace here of the false, and, if one may say so, materialistic philosophy which regards a gun as an evil thing in itself. The wording is in conformity with the Swiss philosophy which he had adopted in regard to military training and with the attitude that he had taken up on the freedom of the seas.

How then, the reader may well ask, did the first draft, conceived, as it was, on sound and sensible lines, come out of the Peace Conference in a form which led to so much mischief in the future? The answer is that the subject fell into inexperienced hands. It must never be forgotten, in considering the Covenant of the League of Nations, that the Prime Ministers of Great Britain and France, the two leading European Powers in the Peace Conference, did not attach sufficient importance to the League of Nations project to find time to attend the Commission which drafted the Covenant. Nor did they even send their foreign ministers or other responsible cabinet members. The representatives who attended in their stead were indeed men of high character and great distinction, but they did not come with the weight of responsibility on their shoulders. The same is true of the representatives of the lesser states who were added to the Commission. Thus it is not surprising, in view of the state of public opinion at that time, especially in the English-speaking countries, that the popular delusion about armaments found its way into the Commission and that Woodrow Wilson failed to make headway against it.

We may conclude our treatment of this subject with an extract from one of Woodrow Wilson's speeches in the closing months of his activity, an address delivered at Sioux Falls, South Dakota, on September 8, 1919:

> We cannot do without force, you cannot establish land titles and not maintain them. Suppose that the land titles of South Dakota were disturbed. Suppose the farm lines were moved, say, ten feet. You know what would happen. Along every fence line you would see farmers perching with guns on their knees. The only reason they are not perching now is that there are land deeds deposited in a particular place, and the whole majesty and force and judicial system of the State of South Dakota are behind the

titles. Very well, we have got to do something like that internationally. You cannot set up Poland, whom all the world through centuries have pitied and sympathized with, as the owner of her property and not have somebody take care that her title-deeds are respected. You cannot establish freedom, my fellow citizens, without force and the only force you can substitute for an armed mankind is the concerted force of the combined action of mankind through the instrumentality of all the enlightened governments of the world."

Admiral Mahan, whose thought was very close to Mackinder's, put the same idea in a telling phrase: "The true function of force is to give moral ideas time to take root."

CHAPTER 33: *Self-Determination*

THE mention of Poland forms an appropriate introduction to another vital element in Woodrow Wilson's thought—that which he crystallized in the watchword "self-determination." No part of his thought has had more momentous consequences, especially in regions of the world where it cannot be taken for granted that the practical application of this watchword will lead to the assumption of political power by what he termed "enlightened governments."

There is an inherent dilemma here with which Woodrow Wilson manfully grappled while he was trying to arrive at a satisfactory formula:

1. Peace requires that men and nations should enjoy a sense of security under the Rule of Law (like the South Dakota farmers mentioned in the preceding chapter).

2. If such a sense of security is not to rest upon armed force alone and if it is to be provided impartially for all states, the small as well as the great, it must rest upon a general system of mutual guarantees of territorial integrity and political independence.

3. But such a general system of guarantees would have the effect of enclosing the family of nations in a strait jacket and interfering with the process of social change—a process which must sooner or later be reflected in political arrangements.

Woodrow Wilson realized that the problem thus raised was insoluble except on the highest political level—that is to say, through the setting up of some international body which would review such situations as impartially as was humanly possible and ensure that any changes in the existing order would take place under the Rule of Law.

Let us now look at the problem as it presented itself to Woodrow Wilson's mind.

In his speech of May 27, 1916, before the League to Enforce Peace he used these words:

> We believe these fundamental things: first, that every people has a right to choose the sovereignty under which they shall live . . . second, that the small states of the world have a right to enjoy the same respect for their sovereignty and for their territorial integrity that great and powerful nations expect and insist upon. And, third, that the world has a right to be free from every disturbance of its peace that has its origin in aggression and disregard of the rights of peoples and nations.

This is good American doctrine reminiscent of 1776. But it goes beyond the Declaration of Independence in its use of the word "choose" without any limiting clause. The Fathers of the Constitution never asserted the right to independence in such sweeping terms; indeed, they admitted that "when in the course of human events it becomes necessary for one people to dissolve the political bands which have connected them with another . . . a decent respect for the opinions of mankind" required that some public justification should be offered. In other words, it is not enough for a people to say, like an old-fashioned sovereign, "such is our will and pleasure." What is involved is a public act, an international act, and it calls for an international justification. The first sentence of the Declaration foreshadows a World Authority.

But under what circumstances should such a political change be allowed to take place? This is what Colonel House tried to set down on paper for the President and the result of his efforts, though it is far from solving the problem, at least has the merit of bringing out how exceedingly difficult it is. Here is his suggested formula for an agreed loosening of the strait jacket:

> The Contracting Powers unite in several guarantees to each other of their territorial integrity and political independence, subject, however, to such territorial modifications, if any, as may become necessary in the future by means of changes in present racial conditions and aspirations, pursuant to the principle of self-determination, and as shall also be regarded by three-fourths of the Delegates of the League of Nations as necessary and proper for the welfare of the peoples concerned; recognizing also that all territorial changes involve equitable compensations and that the peace of the world is superior in importance and interest to questions of boundary.

This is as far as Woodrow Wilson proceeded in a theoretical attempt to solve the dilemma. In effect, he admitted that it was, theoretically, insoluble. But he soon found that he had to take up a position on a whole series of practical problems of political change—the problems resulting from the moribund condition of the Austro-Hungarian and Turkish Empires. On these he had provisional solutions to offer which are set forth in his ninth, tenth, eleventh, twelfth, and thirteenth Points. Only in the case of Poland is his endorsement of self-determination specific and unreserved.

CHAPTER 34: *Regional Understandings*

ONE of the most fruitful ideas originated by Woodrow Wilson was the transformation of the Monroe Doctrine into an integral part of a world-wide organization for peace. This reached its final formulation in Article 21 of the League of Nations Covenant, in which the doctrine is specifically mentioned and described as falling into the class of "regional understandings for the maintenance of peace." But behind this lay a story going back to the first year of Woodrow Wilson's Presidency.

On October 27, 1913, when the Panama Canal was approaching completion, Woodrow Wilson made a speech at Mobile, Alabama, before the Southern Commercial Congress in which he drew attention to the new currents of intercourse which would be set running by the opening of the canal. "Do you realize," he asked his business audience, quite in the spirit of Mackinder, "that New York will be nearer the Western Coast of South America than she is now to the Eastern Coast of South America . . . and that a line drawn northward parallel with the greater part of the Western Coast of South America will run only about 150 miles west of New York? The great bulk of South America, if you will look at your globes (not at your Mercator's projection), lies eastward of the continent of North America. . . . The Canal will run southeast, not southwest, and when you get into the Pacific you will be farther East than when you left the Gulf of Mexico."

Starting from this geographical exposition, the President went on to speak on what the intercourse resulting from the canal would mean for the relations between the United States and the peoples of Latin America. "We must prove ourselves their friends and champions upon terms of equality and honor . . . by comprehending their interest whether it squares with our own interest or not." And he brought his thought on this subject to a practical point by criticizing the use of the term "concessions" in connection with the enterprise of United States citizens in Latin American countries. "We do not hear of concessions for foreign capitalists in the United States. They are not granted concessions. They are invited to make investments. It is an invitation and not a privilege. . . . What these states are going to see, therefore, is an emancipation from the subordination, which has been inevitable, to foreign enterprise and an assertion of the splendid character which, in spite of these difficulties, they have again and again been able to demonstrate."

87

This was the first enunciation of a new outlook which it took some years for American statesmen to bring in full practical effect. The definite "shift in policy," as Colonel Stimson calls it in his autobiography, occurred toward the end of the Coolidge administration in 1928 when, after the appointment of Dwight Morrow to be Ambassador to Mexico, the State Department abandoned the so-called "Roosevelt Corollary to the Monroe Doctrine" which, in Stimson's words, "had brought American marines to Nicaragua, an American-written Constitution to Haiti, and American customs collectors to the Dominican Republic." The new policy was set forth in a long memorandum by J. Reuben Clark, published in 1930, when Stimson was the Secretary of State. He himself aptly summed it up in an address, delivered in February, 1931, before the Council on Foreign Relations, in which he declared: "The Monroe Doctrine was a declaration of the United States versus Europe—not of the United States versus Latin America."

This digression was meant to show how the first of the regional understandings for the maintenance of peace, into which the world of 1952 is becoming organized, came into existence and what a change it involved in the modes of thinking prevalent in the United States about Latin America in 1913.

Let us now go on to see how Woodrow Wilson's thinking about Latin America tied in with his general thinking on world affairs.

On December 16, 1914, when the President was pondering over the European War, Colonel House suggested to him that he should "formulate a plan to be agreed upon by the republics of the two Continents, which in itself would serve as a model for the European nations" when the time came for making peace.

Woodrow Wilson at once responded to this idea. He took a pencil, said House, and wrote out the following formula: "mutual guarantees of political independence under republican forms of government and mutual guarantees of territorial integrity," adding a second clause about the control of the manufacture and sale of munitions of war. "He then," says House, "went to his little typewriter and made a copy of what he had written, and handed it to me to use with the three South American ambassadors with whom it was thought best to initiate negotiations."

88

The ensuing negotiations soon ran into difficulties and when the United States entered the war in 1917 the proposed Pan-American Pact was pushed to one side. But the idea he had outlined with his "little typewriter" remained firmly fixed in the President's mind and reappeared in his Fourteenth Point of January 8, when he laid it down that "a general association of nations must be formed under specific covenants for the purpose of affording mutual guarantees of political independence and territorial integrity to great and small states alike." Two months earlier, in conversation with a Swiss visitor, Professor Rappard of Geneva, he had remarked: "What I should like to do for the world is what I unsuccessfully attempted to do for the American Continent a year or two ago."

CHAPTER 35: *International Justice*

A.   THE STATESMEN'S TRIBUNAL

WE have seen in a previous chapter how Woodrow Wilson refused to make any use of the Hague Conference system in preparing the League of Nations Covenant. Elihu Root had done his best to interest him in the subject and it was after consultation with Root that Colonel House put before the President a proposal for "an International Court of not more than fifteen members" on the model of the Permanent Court of Arbitral Justice proposed at The Hague in 1907. But Woodrow Wilson would have none of it. " He has cut out the Court," reported House in his diary on August 15, 1918. "We were in absolute disagreement about this."

Nevertheless, when the text of the Covenant was submitted to the Peace Conference in Paris, it contained an article in the following terms:

> The Council (of the League) shall formulate and submit to the Members of the League for adoption plans for the establishment

89

of a Permanent Court of International Justice. The Court shall be competent to hear and determine any dispute of an international character which the parties thereto submit to it. The Court may also give an advisory opinion upon any dispute or question referred to it by the Council.

This Article, number 14, is sandwiched in between three articles, numbers 12, 13, and 15, dealing with the functions of the League Council in regard to disputes and it has all the appearance of an afterthought; indeed, the text of the Covenant was amended in several places in 1924 to insert references to "judicial settlement," side by side with arbitration and to make specific reference to the Court as the body to which certain classes of disputes are to be referred, unless the parties have agreed to use a different "tribunal." It would seem, therefore, that, though Woodrow Wilson made himself responsible for Article 14, he still adhered to his old position.

Light is thrown on his attitude on the subject by three references which he made to it in speeches during his Western tour in the fall of 1919, just before he became ill. These show that he considered that the Council of the League of Nations, through the jurisdiction which was given to it to deal with disputes, was in fact, in this aspect of its activity, a Court of Arbitral Justice.

In a speech at Billings, Montana, on September 11, 1919, Woodrow Wilson recalled the fact that, in 1915 and in two years following, the two Houses of Congress proposed the setting up of an International Court. They put it in what in another speech on the subject (at Seattle, on September 13) he calls "a very unexpected place namely, in an appropriation bill" and he proceeded to cite the text of the resolution:

The President is authorized and requested to invite at an appropriate time, not later than the close of the war in Europe, all the great governments of the world to send representatives to a conference which shall be charged with the duty of formulating a plan for the court of arbitration or other tribunal to which disputed questions between governments shall be referred for adjustments and peaceful settlement.

In the Seattle speech the President, disregarding the language of Congress, uses the more general term "permanent Court of International Justice" and makes some observations about it: "You know what a Court of International Justice implies. You cannot set up a Court without respecting its decrees. You cannot make a toy of it. You cannot make a mockery of it. If you, indeed, want a Court, then you must abide by the judgments of the Court," but, so he told the Montana audience, "now that they have got it they do not like it."

Does "it" in this last sentence refer to the Court provided for, but not yet set up, under Article 14 of the Covenant, or to the jurisdiction given to the Council of the League in Articles 12, 13, and 15?

This question would seem to be definitely answered in his third speech on the subject, delivered at Coeur d'Alene, Idaho, on September 12. The purpose of the League of Nations, he there tells his fellow citizens:

". . . is to bring about the thing that America has been advocating ever since I was born. It is a League to bring it about that there shall not be war, but that there shall be substituted for it arbitration and the calm settlement of discussion. That is the heart of the League. The heart of the League is this: every member of the League, and that will mean every fighting nation in the world except Germany, agrees that it will never go to war without first having done one or other of two things—either having submitted the matter in dispute to arbitration, in which case it agrees absolutely to abide by the result, or having submitted it to consideration by the Council of the League of Nations, in which case it promises to lay all the documents, all the facts, in its possession before the Council and to give the Council six months in which to consider the matter, and, if it does not like the opinion of the Council at the end of the six months, still to wait three months more before it resorts to arms. That is what America has been striving for. That is what the Congress of the United States directed me to bring about. Perhaps you do not know where: it was in the naval appropriation bill. . . . When I came back with this covenant of the League of Nations, I had fulfilled the mandate of the Congress of the United States; and now they do not like it."

This surely makes it quite clear that it is the League Council, rather than the proposed new Court, to which he was referring in his Seattle speech, when he spoke of the power to make "judgments" by which even the Great Powers "must abide."

It is true that, as Woodrow Wilson explained, the Council procedure still leaves a gap open for war after nine months, but the President was obviously confident that world public opinion, to which he attached great importance, would in that event prove powerful enough to deter any state from breaking the peace. He therefore did not press the defenders of state sovereignty to go the whole length of stigmatizing resort to the breach of the peace as a "crime." In 1919 they were not yet intellectually ready for this.

The conclusion then is that, when he presented the text of the Covenant including Article 14, Woodrow Wilson was prepared to favor the establishment of two Courts—what one might call a Statesmen's Court and a Jurists' Court, one at Geneva and the other at The Hague.

B. THE JURISTS' TRIBUNAL

The story of the Jurists' Court is told in the biography of Elihu Root.

It opens in July, 1919, when the Covenant, including the Statesmen's Court, had been adopted by the Peace Conference and Woodrow Wilson had left Paris with the intention of explaining the result of his mission to Europe to his compatriots.

It was at that time that Sir Eric Drummond, the Secretary-General designate of the League of Nations, and a member of the Organization Committee of the League appointed by the Peace Conference, asked Woodrow Wilson to suggest a distinguished American to serve on an international Committee of Jurists to frame a plan for a Permanent Court of International Justice. The President put forward the name of Elihu Root and in March, 1920, Root received a formal invitation from Sir Eric, now functioning as Secretary-General of the League.

Root's biographer records the sequel. The Committee of Jurists met at The Hague on June 16, 1920, and elected Baron Descamps of Belgium as Chairman and Judge Loder of Holland as Vice-Chairman. The British member was Lord Phillimore. Root took the lead in the discussions. It was he who suggested the solution of the difficulty which had blocked the progress of the plans for the Court of Arbitral Justice at The Hague in 1907. There had been a failure at that time to agree on the method of selecting judges. Should they be chosen by all the states voting as equals or should the voting system be weighted in favor of the Great Powers? The establishment of the League of Nations pointed to a way out of the impasse. Root called attention to the system adopted in framing the Constitution of the United States, when the smaller states were given equal representation in the Senate, while the larger received representation in the House in proportion to the size of their population. He proposed that the Council and Assembly of the League be brought into the plan in a somewhat similar way. The two bodies should vote concurrently, but separately, on a list of nominees and a majority of votes in each body should be required for the election of the judges. Should there be a deadlock, a conference committee of representatives of both bodies should be invoked, on the analogy of the conference committee of the two Houses of Congress. The plan was adopted and remained in use throughout the life of the Court, in spite of the fact that the predominance of the Great Powers in the Council of the League was whittled down in later years until by 1939 there were nine lesser states out of a total of fifteen.

Another matter on which Root took a vigorous line was in regard to the method of nominating candidates for judgeships. He strongly opposed the suggestion that these should be made by governments, considering it of great importance that judges should not be chosen for political reasons, but solely because of their personal qualifications for the office. The plan which he put forward to ensure this was ingenious and turned out to be well adapted for its purpose. He proposed that the national groups on the panel of the Permanent Court of Arbitration of The Hague—eminent persons whose services had not very often been drawn upon—should each make four nominations, not more than two of whom could be of their own nationality. The lists would be combined and then submitted for balloting to the two League bodies.

But more important than these questions of procedure was that of the nature and scope of the Court's jurisdiction. Under the principle of sovereignty it had always been regarded as unthinkable that a state should be summoned into court against its own will, as an individual is summoned into a national court. Root, as we have seen, held an entirely different theory. He was prepared, in his own words, "to make every sovereign state subject to the superior right of a community of sovereign states to have the peace preserved," and, if he was prepared to go that length in matters of vital importance to the states concerned, he was naturally no less ready to set sovereignty aside in the comparatively minor matters on which the litigation of the Court was likely to be engaged. He therefore proposed that, when a matter was submitted to the Court by one party—which under the Court statute must be a state—the Court should be empowered to oblige the other party to appear and defend its case. This is the principle of "obligatory jurisdiction"—a principle which had already begun to make way in bilateral arbitration treaties.

Root succeeded in getting this far-reaching principle adopted in the report of the committee, but, when it was submitted at Geneva to the scrutiny of the Great Powers, it was struck out. In its place the First Assembly inserted a provision allowing any state to make a declaration accepting the obligatory jurisdiction of the Court on terms of reciprocity or otherwise. This is the famous Article 38 in the statute which later played an important part in the history of the Court and of the League, as it could be used by impatient internationalists as a short cut into the world community behind the backs of the peoples concerned. As it was, it was a considerable victory for Root that, thus amended, the plan went through.

Another important provision which Root joined in incorporating in the draft was that authorizing the Court to set forth advisory opinions. This, too, successfully ran the gauntlet, though it was viewed with suspicion by at least one member of the Council.

This was made clear to Root when he later visited Geneva in 1929. On that occasion the Italian representative, Professor Scialoja, told him privately that "the Council found that the Court was too judicial and independent and they could not get the kind of advice they wanted. It was more satisfactory, from his (i.e. Mussolini's) point of view, for the Council to refer questions to a special Committee of Jurists on each occasion." This is, of course, like saying that the United States government would rather see a matter go to its own attorney general than to the Supreme Court. However, since advisory opinions were provided for in the text of Article 14 of the Covenant, there was nothing that the Council could do about it except to make as little use of them as possible.

Another provision in the statute—and one in which Root had his way all along the line—was that, in electing judges, consideration should be given to ensuring the representation of "the main forms of civilization and the principal legal systems of the world." In this, as in the project as a whole, Root enjoyed the close collaboration of Phillimore who, in writing to Root some years later, referred to the new institution as "your and my Court of International Justice." Their collaboration was indeed very necessary in order to ensure that the common law system should hold its own against the Roman-trained lawyers. In a speech to the New York City Bar Association after his return, Root recounted how he and Phillimore had frequently found themselves up against "a granite wall," in the shape of the Continental lawyers, who could not understand the British-American point of view. That granite wall is still there, though it has been somewhat weakened by the collaboration brought about in the working of the Court between the two—and indeed more than two—schools of lawyers represented on it.

At this point it is necessary to look back to our previous discussion on the nature of law.

We have seen that law, which is so potent an influence in American, and also in English, life is intimately bound up with the concept of popular consent that is at the heart of democracy. It is, in words already cited from Justice Holmes (with whom Root was on terms of cordial friendship, and who was there who talked to

Holmes who did not fall under his spell?), "the witness and deposit of the moral life" of the community or, to put it in another way, an overriding social rule—that is, a rule overriding the claims of all other groups and associations in the state. The reason why American and British statesmen, in speaking of world peace, associate it with the Rule of Law is because they hope to transfer to the international realm the deep respect which their peoples feel for *their own law*, with the ethical values that have become bound up with it over the years.

But where does democracy find a place in the amalgam of the Common Law and the Roman Law systems, together with Oriental and other components, which forms the basis of the law of the World Court? Only very indirectly, through the system of national panels, are the judges who interpret it related to the peoples of the states members of the League of Nations. These judges are, no doubt, chosen—and, in the main, well chosen—from the panels already mentioned, and the panels themselves have been equally well chosen by the governments concerned. It is true that there is nothing to ensure that these governments should be democratic, either in form or in reality; but the danger that a well-qualified nominee might be left out in the cold for political or other reasons has been lessened by the requirement, insisted on by Root, that two of the four nominees made by the panels should be non-nationals.

But, even so, the relationship between the new Court set up at The Hague and the peoples whose "law," or laws, it interprets is still extremely tenuous. One cannot sense the surge of social forces beating against the walls of the Peace Palace at The Hague or penetrating into its dignified chamber. An English lawyer, a great devotee of the Court, once remarked to the writer that he hoped to live to see the day when the London *Times* would give as much space to the proceedings at The Hague as it was in the habit of allotting to the British Law Reports. That day still seems distant. Have we the time to wait until custom has accomplished its quiet work? Or must we look to other means to hasten the coming of the Rule of Law?

TWENTY YEARS OF EXPEDIENTS

SECTION VI

TWENTY YEARS OF EXPEDIENTS

Wandering between two worlds, one dead
The other powerless to be born

— MATTHEW ARNOLD

CHAPTER 36: *The Rupture of Confidence*

AFTER Woodrow Wilson returned from Paris with the treaty
of peace with Germany, containing the Covenant of the League
of Nations, there was a long delay, during which the world waited
anxiously for the fulfillment of the hopes and wishes aroused by
the spokesman of the United States. Europeans could not be
expected to understand the intricacies of American party politics
or of the working of the United States Constitution; but they
grew increasingly alarmed, especially as political and economic
conditions continued to be dangerously disturbed. The British
government, concerned at the course which events seemed to be
taking at Washington, sent over the former Foreign Secretary,
who had now become Viscount Grey, on a mission of observation; but the ailing President was unable to receive him and he

99

returned to London after three months with nothing accomplished.

Meanwhile in political circles there was much discussion of "reservations" to be attached to the treaty by the Senate, some far-reaching, others characterized as "mild." Finally, on March 19, 1920, the treaty, with fifteen reservations of a miscellaneous character attached to it, was submitted to the Senate for a second time for ratification by the necessary two-thirds majority. Forty-nine Senators, more than half the whole body, voted in favor and thirty-five against. As this was seven less than the number needed, the treaty failed to secure the necessary "consent," and therewith a new period of world history began.

It is impossible to convey to a later generation the shock that this caused to the peoples of Europe.

It must be remembered that, for a century before 1914, Europeans had been living under what most of them had come to consider as something akin to an unwritten constitution—at least so far as the maintenance of general peace was concerned. The Great Powers were generally regarded as the policemen of the European order. In 1914, to the consternation of the ordinary citizens, these policemen had started fighting among themselves, involving the whole Continent in what, in the interdependent social and economic conditions which had grown up in the long years of peace, was, geographically speaking, a civil war. When the fighting ended, men looked forward to a return to so-called normal conditions of settled peace, fortified by the improvements provided through the new American plan of the League of Nations.

But how was this peace to be insured? Who was there to guarantee it? The "Concert" of the European Great Powers who had presided over the destinies of the Continent, had fallen apart. Austria-Hungary no longer existed and none of the states which had taken over its sprawling territories had either the power or the experience to step into its place. Russia was in chaos. Defeated Germany, though she had become a democracy, at least in form, was under a military occupation and in any case was certainly not a responsible power. Italy was in a state of violent excitement over the question of her northeastern frontiers. Only France and Great Britain remained to resume the old stewardship, reinforced, as everyone expected, by the United States.

And now the Americans had walked out, leaving Europe exhausted and impoverished and forcing the two Western Powers, at short notice, to improvise not solutions but *expedients*, for the mass of problems left upon their hands: territorial problems stretching from Fiume and Danzig to Eastern Galicia and Armenia—not to speak of Shantung—economic problems, including German reparations, where there was now a vacant seat on the Commission set up by the peace treaty, and all the other matters —health, labor, transport, and the like, on which the network of treaties which had regulated the life of Europe before 1914 needed to be reknit and readapted to the changed conditions in Europe and the world as a whole!

During the closing months of the war and during the Peace Conference, Europeans had temporarily recovered their morale, buoyed up as they were by Woodrow Wilson's optimistic outlook and his assurances of American co-operation in the future. But now all these hopes were dashed down, the rosy vision dissolved into thin air and the prospect before the Continent was bleak and desolate.

No doubt, Americans can say, and say with correctitude, that Europeans had no warrant for indulging in such hopes and visions. But it is a fact of history that they did so. When their anticipations were roughly dissipated by the action of the United States Senate, Europeans became victims of what it has become fashionable to describe as a neurosis, a sullen and cynical mood which was the running undercurrent in European statesmanship, especially in France and Great Britain, during the ensuing thirty years, persisting even after the defaulting associate of 1920 had become a bountiful fairy brimming over with helpfulness and good will such as should have been more than sufficient to dispel any memories of doubt and suspicion.

THE United States had disowned its own child, the League of Nations. But the child went on living without its parents.

The Treaty of Versailles stipulated that its provisions would enter into force as soon as it had been ratified "by Germany on the one hand and three of the Principal Allied and Associated Powers on the other hand." This condition was fulfilled on January 10, 1920, two months before the final veto in the United States Senate. When the blow fell, what could Britain and France and the other "Members of the League" do but carry on as best they could? There were 32 "original Members of the League," owing their status to the fact they had signed the Treaty of Peace; in the case of China, who refused to sign the German Treaty, because of the Shantung question, signature of the Austrian Treaty did duty for the occasion. There were also 13 states "invited to accede" to the Covenant; these were states which had been neutral in the war.

Careful arrangements had been made during the previous year to prepare the League machinery and the new institutions were rapidly set up. The first meeting of the Council took place on January 10 itself and the first meeting of the Assembly in the following September. Meanwhile the Secretary-General, Sir Eric Drummond, an experienced British official with nineteen years of foreign office service behind him, had been busy in picking the best men that he could find for the secretariat—and an excellent team they were. There was nothing to prevent his extending invitations to citizens of the United States. Mr. Raymond Fosdick, who had been the chief civilian adviser of the American Commander in Chief in France, was offered the post of Under-Secretary-General, which he felt himself unable to hold after the Senate's action; other Americans accepted posts on a somewhat lower level and continued to occupy them for many years. This was at a time when the State Department, mistaking the American eagle for an ostrich, pretended to be unaware that the Senate's veto did not extend beyond the water's edge. Relics of this curious state of mind persisted for many years. It fell to the writer, some time in the middle twenties, to receive at Geneva a leading Republican noted for his active interest in international institutions. He will never forget how, when he was on his way to the League building, the distinguished personage remarked, without a trace of any redeeming twinkle in his eye, "And now let us proceed to the *Association of Nations.*"

The world of the twenties, however, needed American experience, American enterprise and initiative, and what is now commonly described as "know-how" as much as it needs them today: and it was not long before means were found of mobilizing them. The vacant chair in the Reparations Commission was filled by an American, first by Mr. Roland W. Boyden and later by Mr. Walter P. Cooke of Buffalo. They bore the honorable title of "United States Citizen Representative" on the Commission; only government representatives could cast a vote, but this hardly diminished their personal influence: for the spirit of the whole United States was present in these able and devoted men. This was the beginning of an association between the United States and the European Powers concerned with reparations which was continued through the collaboration of Charles G. Dawes and two Americans who rendered memorable service in the administration of the Dawes Plan in Berlin, Parker Gilbert and George P. Auld, and later through Owen D. Young; fine service of a similar kind was rendered by Jeremiah Smith in Hungary. Many other individual Americans worked manfully during these years to make amends for their government's sins of omission. It would be invidious to make an enumeration, but there are some names which cannot be omitted, as they belong to the history of our subject. The contribution made by David Hunter Miller to our knowledge of the Paris Peace Conference, and of the drafting of the League of Nations Covenant in particular, has been invaluable to students of contemporary history, as it will always continue to be. Another notable service in a different field, that of Mackinder, was rendered by Isaiah Bowman in his book *The New World*, with its masterly presentation, renewed in successive editions, of the world as it was in the years following the Paris Peace Conference. Three other names which European students of contemporary history hold in especial honor are those of James Brown Scott, who through his studies on international law and diplomacy and through his strongly-marked and engaging personality laid a whole generation of students in his debt; of Archibald Cary Coolidge, the first editor of *Foreign Affairs*, who set a standard for that quarterly periodical which was, and remains, a challenge to all others in that field; and of James T. Shotwell, whose constructive labors in connection with the Geneva Protocol of 1924 and the Briand-Kellogg Pact of 1929 have earned for him a special niche in the temple of the peacemakers.

CHAPTER 38: *Europe Gropes Her Way Without America*

IT would carry us too far to trace the course of international politics in Europe during the twenty-one years between the close of World War I and the opening of World War II. A brief summary must suffice.

That period divides itself sharply into two phases. The first was the phase of British-French hegemony which arose out of the Peace Conference and ended with the evacuation of the Rhineland by the French and British forces in 1929 and the startling first successes of the National Socialists in the German elections which followed almost immediately after. It is perhaps misleading to describe these years as a period of dual hegemony, since the two Powers were in fundamental disagreement all the time and their open bickering was all too frequent. Ramsay MacDonald in 1923-24 and Austen Chamberlain in the following years, each in his own way, did their best to improve relations, as did Herriot and Briand on the opposite side of the Channel. But the two public opinions had taken up fixed positions and the debates in the Geneva Assembly and Commissions came to resemble the trench warfare of World War I.

The second phase included the economic crisis resulting from the depression in the United States, the rise of Hitler to power, the nullification of the military clauses of the Treaty of Versailles, with the German reoccupation of the Rhineland, and the achievement of German hegemony in Eastern Europe through control over Austria and Czecho-Slovakia.

In the course of these events, during which Hughes, Kellogg, Stimson, and Cordell Hull were successively Secretaries of State, the United States government was continuously active behind the scenes and intervened openly from time to time: one need only mention the Hoover Moratorium. But, in the prevailing state of American public opinion, no systematic policy was possible.

From the point of view of these pages, the chief interest of those years lies in the proceedings of the League of Nations. For, though this institution never developed the authority to which Woodrow Wilson hoped and expected that it would attain, it was functioning all the time in the many fields assigned to it in the Covenant and gathering invaluable experience. It was, in fact, a laboratory of political science—all the more useful for students, perhaps, because it was not in the spotlight and its experiments could therefore be carried out under relatively favorable conditions. It is unnecessary to summarize the contribution of Geneva at this stage of our inquiry, since we shall be making full use of it at a later stage.

CHAPTER 39: *The Far-Eastern Object Lesson*

THE United States felt no inclination to take an active part in European affairs. The natural instinct of the American people has been, as there is no need to repeat, not to be involved in the complexities of these problems. But this allergic disposition did not exist in the case of the Far East, where, for the three generations preceding 1919, American diplomacy and individual American pioneers had been active, notably in the mission field. When Americans looked across the Pacific, they did so with a good conscience and with legitimate pride.

Thus it is not surprising that the first major task undertaken by the United States government in world affairs after the Paris Peace Conference should have been concerned with the Far East.

As the events which took place in this connection turned out to be something like a model object lesson, it will be necessary to deal with them in some detail; for they enable us to see American statesmanship attempting to conduct foreign policy in accordance with traditional American ideas and standards, but without the support of a fixed and regular system, such as the League of Nations would have supplied. Only by a close analysis of the many factors involved can one arrive at an understanding of the Washington Conference as part of "that extraordinary movement," as it has been called, "by which the partners of one great war disarmed each other in the short period which remained before they were to be partners again in an even greater war."

One of the reservations attached by the Senatorial opponents to President Wilson's Treaty of Peace with Germany withheld the assent of the United States to the clauses in the treaty relating to Shantung, leaving the United States with complete liberty of action in this question.

The Shantung clauses of the treaty were rightly unpopular in American eyes, for they prolonged the Japanese occupation of that Chinese province which the American people, in harmony with their political traditions, desired to see returned to China. But, as President Wilson patiently explained on repeated occasions to audiences of his fellow citizens, it was not Japan who had seized this province from China. It was Germany who had seized it from China many years before, in the bad old days when every

Power took what it could, and William McKinley and John Hay, the President and Secretary of State at that time, in the existing state of international law, "did not feel at liberty to make even a protest" against the German action. Thus, when Japan, after entering the war, seized the province in her turn, she was doing no wrong in the light of the prevailing diplomatic rules. Therefore to ask her to return the province to China was to ask her to go out of her way to play the part of good neighbor. This, though it might seem to Americans the proper and natural thing to do, was not at all in accordance with Japanese political standards at that time. The task of Woodrow Wilson in trying to carry out American wishes in this matter was made more embarrassing because of a secret arrangement made by Great Britain and, later by France, before the United States entered the war. In order to make it more certain that Japan would declare war on Germany and so join in clearing the Pacific of German ships, these two Powers had promised that any rights that Germany possessed in China should, in the event of victory of the Allies, be transferred to Japanese hands.

An additional difficulty in the President's relations with Japan was the fact that, during the discussions on the drafting of the Covenant, he had felt bound to take a stand against the insertion into the document of a phrase endorsing the principle of "racial equality." This had been a bitter disappointment to the Japanese, and caused an immediate hardening of their attitude on other issues.

In spite of these adverse conditions, Woodrow Wilson had nevertheless succeeded in inducing the Japanese government to abandon the sovereign rights which Germany had enjoyed in Shantung, retaining only what other nations had already been given elsewhere: economic rights in connection with railroads and mines. As the President explained, this was the best bargain he could secure and, if the American people would not agree to it, the only other way to get the province back for China would be by war—a war from which Britain and France would probably stand aside.

After the veto in the Senate, the German Treaty and with it the Shantung clauses remained unratified, leaving this and other Far Eastern problems in the air. Meanwhile, other troubles were accumulating in that region, affecting not only Japan and China, but also Great Britain. Japan had taken advantage of the war as early as May, 1915, to press on China a number of claims known as the Twenty-One Demands, seriously infringing Chinese independence. After the United States entered the war, the Japanese government had sent Viscount Ishii on a special mission to Washington. This led to an agreement—the so-called Lansing-Ishii Agreement—in which the United States government recognized that, owing to "territorial propinquity," Japan had "special interests" in China, "particularly in the part to which her possessions are contiguous." These special interests were not defined in the agreement. Ishii interpreted them as *political* interests and claimed in Tokyo to have won a diplomatic victory. Lansing on the other hand interpreted the word as referring merely to *economic* interests, saying that to recognize a special interest created by geographical propinquity was "an axiom and nothing more." At the end of Woodrow Wilson's Presidency, this highly important issue was left unsettled.

There was also friction between the two Powers owing to the presence of Japanese troops in Siberia. They had gone there by agreement between the Chinese and Japanese governments—nominally, in order to assist Czecho-Slovak forces which had made their way eastward in their effort to evacuate Bolshevik territory. This had led in its turn to the sending of a small United States expedition to Vladivostok. Japan had agreed to evacuate all troops from Siberian territory when the Czecho-Slovaks had been relieved. Nevertheless, the Japanese were still in Siberia in 1921.

Last, but not least, there was the question of naval competition, an inevitable accompaniment of the political tension. The United States had emerged from the war as, potentially, the greatest naval power; but neither Great Britain nor Japan relished this fact. Writers on naval affairs pointed out that, at the rate at which the naval progress of the three powers was then going forward,

Japanese naval power would reach its peak in 1923. That year therefore "loomed ahead as a possible date for war."

A further element in this complex political situation was the fact that Japan and Great Britain were joined in an alliance dating back to 1902. This had been renewed for ten years in 1911, to continue after the decade subject to abrogation by either side at one year's notice. During the summer of 1921 an imperial conference took place in London in which Canada opposed the renewal of the alliance, which, technically speaking involved the risk of hostilities between Great Britain and the United States. In this connection, Great Britain had persuaded Japan to make a joint statement with her to the League of Nations on July 8, 1920, that the alliance, "though in harmony with the spirit" of the Covenant, "was not entirely consistent with its letter" and that the two parties recognized that, if renewed, it must be put in a form consistent with the Covenant.

Such was the condition of affairs with which the administration that came into power early in 1921 found itself confronted. It was evidently necessary to take action and the only means available to the United States, since she had isolated herself from Geneva, was through an international conference of the conventional nineteenth-century type. The newly-elected President therefore sent out a call for a conference to meet at Washington. The Powers invited included "the Principal Allied and Associated Powers," i. e. France, Great Britain, Italy, and Japan—Russia was not included because she had severed her connection with the other Powers after the Revolution. China was, of course, invited too, as also Holland, Belgium, and Portugal, because of their respective interests in the Far East.

The day of meeting was fixed for November 11, 1921, Armistice Day. The conference lasted for nearly three months, adjourning on February 6, 1922.

The Washington Conference was hailed at the time as a great diplomatic success for the United States. Let us look at it in the perspective of thirty years.

What attracted the chief attention in the West were the naval clauses. We will therefore deal first with these.

The Secretary of State startled his colleagues at the conference and electrified the whole world by proposing, at the first session, that "preparations for offensive war stop now." He then put forward a detailed program for the reduction of battleships according to an agreed ratio, which was adopted by the conference with slight modifications and embodied in a special treaty. The ratio was as follows: The United States 5, Great Britain 5, Japan 3, France 1.7, Italy 1.7. The treaty also provided for the sinking or scrapping of designated ships, built or in construction, of the three leading naval powers and a naval holiday in the construction of capital ships for ten years, with only limited replacements of superannuated ships thereafter until 1936.

Side by side with these provisions for the reduction of naval armaments, the treaty provided for important limitations of fortification as follows:

The United States agreed to maintain the existing position in the insular possessions which it held at that time, or might acquire thereafter, in the Pacific Ocean, except (a) those adjacent to the coast of the United States, Alaska, and the Panama Canal Zone, not including the Aleutian Islands, and (b) the Hawaiian Islands.

Great Britain agreed to maintain the *status quo* in Hongkong and the insular possessions which the British Empire now held or might thereafter acquire in the Pacific Ocean, east of the meridian of 110 east longitude (this meridian runs just East of Singapore) except (a) those adjacent to the coast of Canada, and (b) the Commonwealth of Australia and its Territories, and New Zealand.

Japan agreed to maintain the *status quo* in the following insular territories and possessions of Japan in the Pacific Ocean, namely: the Kurile Islands, the Bonin Islands, the Loochoo Islands, Formosa, and the Pescadores, and any insular territories or possessions in the Pacific Ocean which Japan might thereafter acquire.

The political effect of these disarmament and nonfortification provisions was, in the words of a leading American authority on the diplomatic history of the United States, "to make it impossible for either one of the three navies alone to fight an offensive war against one of the others in the Pacific." Thus, he continues, "Japan secured the impregnability of her own islands to any attack from Pacific waters, and established an irresistible dominance of her power in Eastern Asia." The same authority, writing in 1937, sums up the conference as a "face-saving retreat of the United States from active diplomacy in the Far East under the cover of a multilateral international agreement for the observance of the traditional American policies" in that area.

It is to this agreement, or rather agreements—for there were several—that we must now turn.

By the disarmament clauses Japan had secured for herself a free hand in China. More than that, as the event showed, she had also secured a free hand over the whole of Eastern Asia, on which she could now look as her own exclusive preserve, or "Co-prosperity Sphere," as she was later ironically to describe it. Some of her leaders even went so far as to compare her policy there with the Monroe Doctrine— a Monroe Doctrine without any of the guarantees of American freedom.

What did she promise to do in exchange?

1. She made a separate Treaty with China for the speedy return of Shantung, subject to the inviolability of private contracts and the purchase by China, in installments, of the former German railroad there.

2. She promised that she would abandon the claim in the Twenty-One Demands for the employment of "influential Japanese by the Chinese government as advisers in political, financial, and military affairs" and to annul the Lansing-Ishii Agreement of 1917. This was formally annulled by an exchange of notes on April 14, 1923.

3. She renewed her pledge to evacuate Siberia. This took place, in October, 1922.

4. She restored the northern half of Sakhalin to Russian sovereignty, after receiving certain economic concessions there and in Siberia. This transaction was only concluded in 1925.

5. She recognized American cable rights on Yap Island.

6. Finally and most important of all, she became a signatory to two regional treaties embodying the constructive labors of the conference as a whole—a Four-Power Treaty "relating to armaments" and a Nine-Power Treaty "relating to principles and policies concerning China."

These Treaties embodied one important principle of the League of Nations Covenant, the principle of *obligatory consultation*. Thus the Four-Power Treaty provided for "a joint Conference" and the Nine-Power Treaty for "full and frank communication." It may be well to quote the exact words of Article 7 of the Nine-Power Treaty:

The Contracting Powers agree that, when a situation arises which, in the opinion of any one of them, involves the application of the stipulations of the present Treaty and renders desirable discussion of such application, there shall be full and frank communication between the Contracting Powers concerned.

So far as it went, this was an excellent statement. But what guarantee was there that it, and the corresponding "joint conference" in the armaments treaty, would be carried out? None whatever, as the League of Nations Mandates Commission discovered in attempting to deal with reports that the Japanese were fortifying their mandated islands in the Pacific—reports that, as the American people learned at precious cost twenty years later, were all too true. For the treaties rested solely on the good faith of the signatories. They were not *institutionalized* by being part of the regular machinery of the League of Nations; and their own provisions, as Stimson ruefully discovered ten years later, were "without teeth." They provided for no action against a violator of their provisions. They were no better, or, as some might prefer to say, no worse than gentlemen's agreements.

This was explicitly set forth by the President in the speech in which he laid the conference treaties before the Senate. "It has been said," he remarked, with a side glance at the League of Nations, "that these are mere meaningless treaties and therefore valueless. Let us accept no such doctrine of despair as that. If nations may not establish by mutual understanding the rules and principles which are to govern their relationship; if a sovereign and solemn plight by the leading nations of the earth is valueless; if nations may not trust one another, then indeed, there is little of which to hand (*sic*) our faith in advancing civilization or the furtherance of peace." And then he proceeded to state the two alternatives between which alone the American people at that time considered itself free to choose. "Either we must live and aspire and achieve under a free and common understanding among peoples, with mutual trust, respect, and forbearance, and exercising full sovereignty, or else brutal armed force will dominate and the sorrows and burdens of war in this decade will be turned to the chaos and hopelessness of the next."

Little did he dream how his words would read thirty years later.

But we must return to the immediate results of the conference.

It is true that the treaties, as also the twelve resolutions adopted, provided opportunities which might have been used for continued co-operation among the Powers, had they chosen to avail themselves of them. Several of these related to reforms in China, including the abolition of extraterritoriality, toward which the signatories declared themselves to be "sympathetically disposed" and for which a commission of inquiry was to be set up. Others merely set forth desirable objectives without even the suggestion of machinery for attaining them. Thus the "Resolution regarding Foreign Postal Agencies in China" provided for their abandonment subject to the condition "that an efficient Chinese postal service is maintained" and in the "Resolution regarding unification of railways in China" the Powers record their "hope that to the utmost degree consistent with existing rights, the future development of railways in China shall be so conducted as to enable the Chinese government to effect the unification of railways into a railway system under Chinese control."

All these were natural and very proper applications of the traditional American policy in China—the Open Door and the administrative and territorial integrity of the country. But, since there was no regular occasion provided for continued contact between the signatories, they lost touch with one another and the wheels of diplomacy revolved with exasperating slowness. It was not till 1929 that, as a result of the Treaty of 1921, China secured fiscal autonomy and was able to put into effect a tariff of her own making. As for extraterritoriality, to which Chinese public opinion attached the greatest importance, the international Commission of Inquiry provided for it at Washington did not meet till 1926 and subsequent progress on the part of the major Powers in carrying its recommendations into effect was so dilatory that in January, 1930, the Chinese abandoned the system by unilateral action.

Meanwhile, Sino-Japanese relations were steadily deteriorating and there was mounting evidence of a fixed determination on the Japanese side to prevent the Chinese government from consolidating its power and effecting the reforms which the American negotiators in 1922 had outlined.

Finally, ten years after the conference, the test of the Washington treaties came in the "Manchurian Incident" of September 18, 1931. But by this time their consultative clauses, for all their "sovereign and solemn plights," had receded into the background, and what stood out in the public mind was the plain and glaring fact that the Japanese had violated the Covenant of the League of Nations.

It so happened that in those September days the Council and Assembly of the League were both in session and that China had just been re-elected a member of the Council. So the stage seemed to be set. The tribunal was there ready at Geneva; and there were the parties.

Action was not slow to follow. Thus already on September 21 the Chinese government appealed to the Council of the League, and, as Stimson puts it, "jurisdiction of the controversy thus passed promptly and properly to the League of Nations, of which the United States was not a member."

The Chinese government certainly acted "promptly": whether it acted "properly" or wisely is open to question, for, despite the letter of the Covenant, the League was no better equipped with "teeth" than the Nine-Power Treaty. Perhaps the object lesson would have been more effective, so far as the American people was concerned, had the emphasis been laid from the beginning on the Nine-Power Treaty rather than on the League Covenant. However that may be, the result would have been equally disastrous: for the American people was unschooled in strategic thinking and needed the bitter lesson of Pearl Harbor in order to realize what it meant to have given Japan a free hand in Eastern Asia and the Northwestern Pacific.

Stimson's autobiography gives a vivid picture of the situation in the Cabinet at that time, with the spirit of Theodore Roosevelt, embodied in the Secretary of State, at odds with the spirit of William Penn in the person of President Hoover. "Each new Japanese aggression," writes Stimson, "stimulated discussion. Thus on October 9, after the bombing of Chinchow, . . . Mr. Hoover expressed the tentative view that the baby must not be deposited on the Americans by the League . . . and warned against getting in a humiliating position in case Japan refused to do anything about what he called our scraps of paper or paper treaties." Stimson's diary continues:

. . . the question of the "scrap of paper" is a pretty crucial one. We have nothing but "scraps of paper." The fight has come on in the worst part of the world for peace treaties. The peace treaties of modern Europe made out by the Western nations of the world no more fit the three great races of Russia, Japan, and China who are meeting in Manchuria than, as I put it to the Cabinet, a stovepipe hat would fit an African savage. Nevertheless they are parties to these and the whole world looks to see whether the treaties are good for anything or not, and if we lie down and treat them as scraps of paper, nothing will happen, and in the future the peace movement will receive a blow that it will not recover from for a long time. Such a course was unthinkable.

"Whatever they might be to other statesmen or to other nations," Stimson's biographer continues, "the treaties were not scraps of paper to Stimson. Respect for treaties was the very foundation of peace. Yet what could he do? The treaties to which the United States government was a party, unlike the Covenant of the League, were treaties without teeth. More important still, since the basic requirement of policy is that it must be supported by public approval and executive leadership, the American government was without teeth. Mr. Hoover was a profoundly peaceable man. Outraged as he was by Japanese aggression, he was opposed, in every fiber of his being to any action which might lead to American participation in the struggles of the Far East. In this view he had the support of American people."

What about economic action to halt the Japanese? Stimson considered this too, but he felt bound to conclude that "anything more than verbal action to check Japanese aggression might well lead to war." The same view was held in London, where the effect of the obligation not to fortify Hongkong weighed heavily in the minds of the responsible authorities. But, if the American government, continues Stimson, "would not condone the tearing up of the treaties, and if it would not take any economic or military action to defend them, what would the American government do?" It was this question which produced the famous nonrecognition doctrine as the only available answer.

At this point in the record we must pause, in order to introduce another factor in the peace movement, which figured in the events that followed.

WE have seen that, after the rejection of the League of Nations Covenant by the Senate, public opinion in the United States remained unsettled and ill at ease. Instead of experiencing a sense of liberation at having cut themselves loose from the affairs of Europe, Americans were haunted by a sense of duty somehow neglected or evaded. This condition of what may be called "balked idealism" left the American people ready to respond to a fresh initiative taken by the peace movement, provided only that this had nothing to do with the League of Nations. Indeed, such a new effort had all the more chance of exerting a powerful influence on public opinion if it went further than the League of Nations Covenant, in which Woodrow Wilson had been forced to yield on important points to the traditional methods and standards of European diplomacy.

It was against this background that, in the years following the defeat of the League in the Senate, a movement was launched in the Middle West for "the outlawry of war."

The object of the proponents of the outlawry of war was very simple. It was to bring the problem of international relations closer to the people by fixing *sole* attention on the subject of war. It aimed at disentangling war from the mass of detail with which particular wars are always associated, and so putting *war in itself*, war alone, in the spotlight, concentrating upon it the whole force of public opinion—particularly religious opinion. Already, under the influence of American pilgrims to Geneva, Geneva delegates were beginning to open their minds to the concept, so much at variance with the traditional "Law of Nations," that war is a *crime*, an offense against the modern social order. The preachers of outlawry went further: they denounced it as a *sin*.

The American pilgrims to the League of Nations Assembly of 1924, acting of course, on an unofficial basis, had submitted to that body, for discussion in the relevant committee, a paper bearing the title "Proposals of the American group" and opening with the words, "Declaration Outlawing Aggressive War." High hopes had been raised by a conversation between Professor Shotwell and Monsieur Herriot, the French Prime Minister, at Lyons a few days before the Assembly opened. But these expectations were disappointed, as the paper never reached the stage of being discussed in the committee. There was nothing to be done but to await a more favorable opportunity.

This presented itself sooner than might have been anticipated. In April, 1927, the tenth anniversary of the entry of the United States into the war was approaching. Why should not the occasion be used to launch the outlawry movement in Europe? This was the idea which Professor Shotwell lodged in the receptive mind of Monsieur Briand. So on April 6, 1927, that statesman addressed a message to the people of the United States saying that "France would be willing to subscribe publicly with the United States to any mutual engagement to outlaw war, to use an American expression, as between these two countries."

A few weeks later, on June 20, this general statement was followed up by a formal diplomatic approach, when the United States Ambassador in Paris was handed by Monsieur Briand a draft treaty in two short articles, outlawing war as between these two countries. After some delay Secretary of State Kellogg replied on December 28, 1927, accepting the French statesman's suggestion and proposing further that France and the United States should join "in an effort to obtain the adherence of the principal Powers of the world to a declaration renouncing war as an instrument of national policy." This led to a long and complicated exchange of views, in which all the principal Powers took part. Eventually the pact was signed in Paris on August 27, 1928, in the form originally proposed by Monsieur Briand and came into force on July 24, 1929, the date of the deposit of the Japanese ratification in Washington. States other than the original signatories hastened to "adhere" to it, and within a few years those who had so bound themselves exceeded in number the members of the League of Nations.

In spite of all that has happened between 1929 and 1952 the pact is still in force, for, as was pointed out at the time by a leading authority, there was no means provided by which the signatories could rid themselves of their obligation. It was "for ever and for ever." One could not "unrenounce" war—at least in words.

Here are the two articles to which allusion has already been made:

1. The high contracting parties solemnly declare in the names of their respective peoples that they condemn recourse to war for the solution of international controversies, and renounce it as an instrument of national policy in their relations with one another.

2. The high contracting parties agree that the settlement or solution of all disputes or conflicts of whatever nature or whatever origin they may be, which may arise between them, shall never be sought except by pacific means.

CHAPTER 41: *Nonrecognition*

HENRY L. Stimson became Secretary of State in March, 1929. No one was more aware than he that the Kellogg Pact, judged by its letter, was no more than "a scrap of paper." But Stimson was a determined man who made use of any tool that came to his hand and he decided to make the most of this latest addition to the armory of peace, however ineffective it might appear to be.

At first fortune favored him and he met with an unexpected success. In the summer of 1929, just when the pact was entering into force, trouble arose between China and the Soviet Union over their respective rights and interests in Northern Manchuria. The Soviet government, in accordance with time-honored power-political methods, sent its troops into Chinese territory and it looked for a while as though the outcome would be either a regular Soviet-Chinese war or a Soviet annexation of Northern Manchuria. At that time the United States had no diplomatic relations with the Soviet Union. Nevertheless, Stimson took the lead in placing the issue on the international plane and invoking the Kellogg Pact, calling on both nations to respect its provisions. This, as Stimson dryly remarks, "greatly annoyed" the Soviet authorities, "whose self-righteousness in foreign affairs makes that of all other nations seem mild indeed." However, their troops were soon withdrawn and the matters in dispute were peacefully settled. To what extent the Kellogg Pact, as a weapon at the disposal of American diplomats, contributed to this result there was no means of judging. But this first encounter strengthened the belief of those who thought that, in resolute hands, the pact could become an effective instrument in the cause of world peace, side by side with the Covenant of the League of Nations.

Indeed, advocates of peace were so much encouraged that hopes were entertained in Geneva circles that the two documents could be harmonized and made into one and the disaster of 1920 thus repaired. An attempt to achieve this was made in the League Assembly of 1929, but it encountered a number of obstacles of a more or less technical nature, and had to be abandoned.

We must now pick up the thread dropped at the end of Chapter thirty-nine.

In the Far Eastern crisis of 1931-32, in which Stimson was unable to use the Covenant of the League of Nations, he saw an opportunity to reinforce the authority of the Nine-Power Washington Treaty by associating it with the Kellogg Pact.

We have already had a glimpse of the Cabinet meeting which followed the Japanese occupation of Chinchow in October, 1931, and of the perplexity in which the President and the Secretary of State were placed. As the Japanese aggression in Manchuria proceeded and American public opinion became more and more disturbed, Stimson decided to take the strongest action available to him within the limits set by the President's fixed determination not to risk involving the United States in war. This took the form of a combination of the doctrine of nonrecognition and the Kellogg Pact.

On January 7, 1932, a note was sent both to China and Japan in the course of which they were notified that the United States did not:

. . . intend to recognize any treaty or agreement entered into between those governments, or agents thereof, which may impair the treaty rights of the United States . . . and that it does not intend to recognize any situation, treaty, or agreement which may be brought about by means contrary to the covenants and obligations of the Pact of Paris of August 27, 1928, to which treaty both China and Japan, as well as the United States, are party.

The nonrecognition doctrine thus set forth, originated, as Stimson records, in a suggestion made by President Hoover two months before. The President's idea was that the best way to meet the Japanese aggression was not by physical resistance but by refusing to legalize the fruits of aggression.

As Stimson saw it, this policy had three advantages. Firstly, it cleared the conscience of the American people in regard to China. Stimson had a keen sense of "the incalculable harm which would be done . . . if, after having for many years assisted by public and private effort in the education and development of China toward the ideals of modern Christian civilization, and having taken the lead in the movement which secured the covenant of all the great powers to respect her sovereignty, her independence, and her territorial and administrative integrity, the United States "should now abandon her to her fate when this same covenant was violated." The United States "might not be able to prevent aggression in China, but she must certainly make her opinion of it clear."

The second advantage, in Stimson's eyes, was that it enabled him to reinforce the Kellogg Pact. "Nonrecognition might not prevent aggression," but to recognize the Japanese action would be to give official authorization to "the use of war as an instrument of national policy."

His third reason was that it was imperative to "give expression to the deep and genuine feeling of the American people, and their Government, that what the Japanese were doing in Manchuria was terribly wrong." In feeling as he did about this Stimson was in line with a deep-rooted sentiment in British public opinion, first voiced by Oliver Cromwell in his protest against the massacre of the Waldensians in the Italian Alps and reiterated in more recent times by Gladstone.

These secondary objects Stimson achieved, so far as words could go, and his gallant initiative will always have an honored place in the annals of American statesmanship. But in his major practical effort to vindicate the Washington treaties in the Far East and thus to reinforce the whole structure of international order, he failed; for, as he sadly records, the note of January 7 "did not win the prompt adherence of any other major power"—not even that of Great Britain. As a result, "the collective peace machinery"—the League Covenant, the Kellogg Pact, the Washington treaties all combined—"received a blow which made it look entirely ineffective."

It would be a deviation from our subject to recount the rest of the melancholy story, through the setting up of the puppet state of Manchukuo, the despatch by the League of Nations of a commission under Lord Lytton, its report condemning the Japanese action and proposing the creation of an autonomous Manchuria within the Chinese Republic, the adoption of that report by the League Assembly, followed by the resignation of Japan from the League, the continuance of Japan's provocative policy in China culminating in the outbreak of open war between the two Powers in 1938, and the eventual linking up of that war in 1941 with the war between Japan and the United States, as part of World War II which had opened in 1939.

At the time of writing, the Chinese people, after a tenacious resistance carried on along traditional lines against Japanese invasion, lies prostrate and seemingly helpless under the barbarous yoke of the Soviet Union, acting through a body of Chinese agents and disciples. The "sovereignty, independence, and territorial and administrative integrity of China," which the United States and the other signatories of the Nine-Power Treaty pledged themselves at Washington to respect and to consult one another about, may seem to many more distant than ever. But the end of these things is not yet.

CHAPTER 42: *Back to Isolationism*

WE have now reached the year 1933. In that year, says a historian of American diplomacy, writing in 1937:

> The new Democratic Administration of President Franklin D. Roosevelt came into office uncommitted by the Stimson Doctrine. It has made no reiteration of that doctrine. It has committed itself in general to a policy of peace and neutrality which makes it inconceivable that the United States would take upon itself alone the enforcement of the Nine-Power Treaty or the Pact of Paris. There is every indication that this will continue to be the policy of the United States in future administrations.

Professor Bemis then goes on to speak of the Act of Congress of March 1934 providing that, after the lapse of a ten-year period of protection under the United States, the Philippine Islands "shall become an absolutely independent Republic." "This act," he continues, "presages a definite retreat by the United States from all active diplomacy in China. If this is accomplished without complications during the next ten years, it will bring to an end the great aberration of 1898."

That the American people were at that time not indisposed toward this frame of mind may be inferred from the unfavorable response of public opinion to President Roosevelt's speech of October, 1937, proposing a "quarantine" against Japan in the Sino-Japanese War then proceeding, and from the very mild reaction to the bombing of the U.S.N. gunboat *Panay* in Chinese waters in the same year.

Here then our exploration of the American road to world peace during the twenty years between the two world wars may well break off; for the Kellogg Pact was the last attempt made by American statesmanship during that period to grapple with the problem of peace and world order on broad lines and as a whole.

The American Road to World Peace

During the years following 1933 the American people concentrated its attention on domestic issues and watched with detachment the steady deterioration of the situation in Europe, accompanied by the decline of the League of Nations and its loss of such authority at it had gained during the twenties. The reaction of these events upon American opinion was, in the words of the new Secretary of State, "an avalanche of isolationism."

This mood found its clearest expression in the neutrality legislation of 1935-37. This involved the virtual abandonment of the principle of the freedom of the seas, which had been one of the cornerstones of American policy ever since the foundation of the Republic. The new policy was based upon the experience gained in the controversy preceding the entry of the United States into World War I and its provisions were drastic and comprehensive. It forbade American ships in time of war to carry arms, ammunition, or implements of war to a belligerent country. It forbade any vessel, domestic or foreign to take out from American ports "men or fuel, arms, ammunition, implements of war, or other supplies," to belligerent warships or tenders. It declared it unlawful for American citizens to travel under a belligerent flag, except as prescribed by the President. It forbade the arming of American merchant ships trading with belligerent countries.

The effect of this policy, as Stimson, with his habitual courage, argued in a public statement in October, 1937, was "to impose a dead level of neutral conduct on the part of our government between right and wrong, between an aggressor and its victim, between a breaker of the law of nations and the nations who are attempting to uphold the law." He described it as "a policy of moral drift" and declared that, by adopting it, the United States had "gone far toward killing" its "influence upon the progress of the world," while at the same time "endangering its own peace."

This legislation was still in force when World War II broke out and when, in June, 1940, after Hitler had overrun Norway, Denmark, France, Belgium, and Holland, Stimson became Secretary of War in the Roosevelt Administration.

AT this point we must interrupt the historical sequence of events in order to consider a slogan which has been much in vogue in recent times in different countries—the slogan that "the causes of war are economic," a companion to the slogan about armaments with which we have already dealt.

As in the case of armaments, there is a simple answer—that it is just not so. It is indeed *demonstrably* not so, as could be shown by citing many instances of wars which occurred when no important economic issues were involved and by citing other occasions when tension arising out of economic issues did not result in war because this was outweighed by other issues making for peace. If one had to choose between the so-called realists for whom the causes of war are economic and the so-called old-fashioned people for whom the one and only road to *peace* is economic, one would not hesitate to side with the latter. But no one who has eyes to survey the whole field of present-day world affairs would wish to become the slave of either formula.

It is worth while pausing to ask why such a palpable error as that the causes of war are economic has become so prevalent in our day. The answer would seem to be that it is due to a simple confusion of thought arising out of the careless use of the word "economic." If that word is used in the sense in which it has been employed by educated people ever since the day of Adam Smith— not to mention Aristotle—economic activity is undoubtedly one of the chief forms of international co-operation in the modern world and therefore an influence making for understanding and peace. Trade implies trust, as every merchant knows, and the more widespread the trade the larger the network of confidence and the volume of intercourse and good will.

But there is a school of thought which maintains that trade is not a process of exchange based on mutual confidence but a process of robbery and exploitation, part of a struggle for power which has been going on among men ever since the beginning of history. For those who think in this way *everything is economic*, because trade, like everything else in social life, including politics, is part of the incessant and ubiquitous struggle between the exploiter and the exploited.

Those who see life in these terms are entitled to their views. But they should not expect everyone else to agree with them—still less to follow them in putting words, and especially key words in the realm of education, to the very peculiar uses to which they themselves see fit to assign them.

This brief general statement seems necessary as an introduction to the man who, as Secretary of State under President Franklin D. Roosevelt during almost the whole of his long tenure of office, made a gallant and persistent attempt to promote world peace through facilitating and developing the process of economic cooperation.

Cordell Hull can be called a nineteenth-century figure. Whether the generation in which he would have found himself fully in his element lies behind us or, as Woodrow Wilson believed, before us, remains to be seen. However that may be, his particular importance for these pages, apart from his devoted sponsorship of the cause of the United Nations, lies in the fact that he sought to put into practice sound and constructive methods of international economic policy under conditions when it was more than usually difficult to do so and amid interruptions and distractions which would have daunted any one less resolute and single-minded than he proved himself to be.

It his earlier years in public life, as he tells us in his *Memoirs*, Cordell Hull favored "any action or agreement that would lower tariff barriers, whether the agreement was multilateral, signed by many or all nations, whether it was regional, embracing only a few, or whether it was bilateral, embracing only two." When he became Secretary of State in 1933, he found himself confronted with an impending International Economic Conference to be held in London under the auspices of the League of Nations and to participation in which the outgoing President had committed the United States. At first in that conference he was still prepared to

126

use the multilateral method, had the other nations been willing, and the world-wide tariff truce which he had prepared at that time, and saw adopted, was conceived along that line. When the conference had revealed only too clearly that public opinion in no country, not excepting the United States, would back up action on multilateral lines, he turned to what he considered to be the next best method of reducing trade barriers, that of bilateral agreements.

Bilateral agreements may be used in different ways, either to increase world trade or to contract it. The way in which the Secretary of State determined to use them was by associating them with the most-favored-nation policy in its unconditional form. The meaning of this rather misleading technical term is that the parties to the tariff treaty agree beforehand to pass on to all other states with which they are in commercial relations any reductions which they may agree upon between themselves. These reductions are passed on "unconditionally"—that is to say, without asking for an extra favor, a *quid pro quo*, in return. Under this system preferential tariff arrangements are ruled out and their place taken by a system of general nondiscrimination and equality of treatment. One of the Secretary's most hard-earned successes was to secure from Great Britain, in the Lend Lease Agreement of 1942, a pledge of adhesion to these principles. As he saw it, this agreement was "a long step toward the fulfillment of the economic principles for which" he "had been fighting for half a century." It "furnished the pattern for agreements with other countries" and laid the "foundation for all . . . later postwar planning in the economic field."

A bill empowering the executive branch of the government to negotiate bilateral treaties on this basis was introduced into Congress in March, 1934, and passed into law by June. Criticism in Congress was mollified by limiting the duration of the act to three years. What might have been a troublesome and even crippling provision turned out in the event to be an advantage; for by 1937 fourteen treaties had been negotiated with satisfactory results in each case. Moreover, the unconditional system had won approval from experts on the international plane. The act was therefore extended by considerable majorities in both Houses and the same success achieved on its subsequent expirations up to the present time—though never without a struggle: this, however, has been useful as a means of keeping public opinion alive in regard to the wider issues involved.

It has been reproached against the trade agreements that they did not prevent World War II. The answer of course, is that their author never claimed that they were capable of exercising a direct influence in the field of power politics. What he has claimed—and claimed without contradiction—is that what is called economic warfare (that is to say, the transference to the field of economic relations of military methods and standards) "offers constant temptations to use force, or threat of force, to obtain what could have been got through normal process of trade." The economic history of the Old World, not least in its relations with the New, under the mercantilist system, abundantly attests the truth of this judgment. One of the long-range and most potent causes of World War I lay in the departure of the leading Continental European states, above all of Germany, in the eighteen-eighties, from the free trade standards which had been accepted doctrine during the earlier part of the century. It was this that was in the mind of Woodrow Wilson when he proclaimed "the removal of all economic barriers" and "the establishment of an equality of trade conditions" as among the most important elements of world peace. And this must also have been in the mind of those who in 1945 awarded to the retiring Secretary of State the signal honor of the Nobel Peace Prize.

CHAPTER 44: *Consultative Pacts*

IN closing the account of the interwar period we must deal with two issues which, though not directly and formally connected with the problem of world peace, have had a very strong indirect connection with it in recent years and cannot therefore be omitted from this record.

The first of these can be described in general terms as the question of consultation or, more specifically, in the form which it assumed during this particular period, the question of a consultative pact.

It has already been stated that in the Washington treaties of 1922 the United States bound itself to "joint conference" with its partners in one case and "full and frank communication" with them in another. This naturally raised the question why this same principle should not be adopted in its negotiations regarding European questions.

This issue arose sharply on two occasions during these years: in the negotiation of the London Naval Treaty of 1930 and in the disarmament discussions at Geneva in 1933 and 1934.

On the former occasion a report was spread that the United States would be ready to enter into a consultative pact—that is to say, to assume an obligation to consult on issues of international peace and security with the other Power or Powers taking part in the negotiations, as the *quid-pro-quo* for a diplomatic concession. In the case in question, the Power seeking the pledge of consultation was France, and the concession to be offered in return was a reduction in her naval forces.

The United States delegation at the Naval Conference hastened to deny this report. Since its government was already a party to two such pacts, it could not denounce the proposal on the ground of principle. Instead, it extricated itself by issuing a lengthy press release from which the two following sentences are a characteristic extract: "If this demand for security could be satisfied in some other way, then the danger of misunderstanding a consultative pact would be eliminated from an entirely different standpoint. In such a case, the American delegation would consider the matter with an entirely open mind."

In order to recall the political atmosphere in which this incident occurred let us set beside the measured language of the London delegation the following comment of the Chairman of the Foreign Relations Committee of the Senate:

It might be helpful if someone in London would define a consultative pact and then place alongside of this definition a further
definition of a security pact. A consultative pact is a security pact
in disguise. In a security pact you state in the pact what you are
going to do after you have consulted. In a consultative pact you
conceal what you are going to do after you have consulted, but
you will be forced by the logic of the hour to do precisely what
you agreed to do in the security pact.

It was about this time that a conversation took place in Washington which is recorded in Stimson's biography. When Pierre
Laval visited that city in 1931—a Laval who, in Stimson's eyes,
showed no sign of what he was later to become—he asked the
President straight out for a consultative pact, to take effect in the
event of a breach of the Kellogg Pact. Briand had asked this before
him, and met with a refusal. But this time Laval had something to
offer in exchange from the French side, disarmament; he told the
President, says Stimson, that "such a promise (of consultation)
would be taken in France as a great gesture which would help
very much the possibility of any disarmament." Stimson's narra-
tive proceeds: "the President replied at once that he thought it
was a political impossibility." On this Stimson, writing in 1947,
makes the following comment:

Perhaps no major nation was ever asked for a smaller contribution to peace and disarmament. In the light of what had happened in 1917 and happened again in 1941, the American refusal
to "consult" with other nations in the event of threatened war was
nothing short of madness . . . yet there it was; a consultative pact
was indeed a "political impossibility" . . . anything of whatever
nature which implied the slightest responsibility for European
peace was anathema to the American people.

The next episode relates to the year 1933-34, when the political
situation in the United States had undergone a certain change.
During the Presidential election of 1932, there was a movement in
American public opinion for the "implementation" of the Kellogg

Pact. This agitation left its mark on the platforms of both political parties. The Republican party favored "enactment by Congress of a measure that will authorize our government to call, or participate in, an international conference in case of any threat of non-fulfillment of Article 2 of the Treaty of Paris (Kellogg-Briand Pact)." The Democrats demanded that the Kellogg Pact "be made effective by provisions for consultation and conference, in case of threatened violation of treaties."

Fortified by this unusual agreement between the two party platforms, Mr. Norman Davis, as chairman of the American delegation to the disarmament Conference at Geneva, was able to take up a much more definite position. The Conference had opened in January 30, 1933. However, it was not till May 22 that Mr. Davis made his first statement. In this he announced that the United States, as a signatory of the Kellogg Pact, was "willing to consult the other states in case of a threat to peace, with a view to averting conflict." This commitment, on the face of it, did not seem to go very far. Nevertheless, at that particular juncture, it was, in the words of an eminent American jurist, "of enormous importance," since it indicated that, under the specified circumstances, the United States would waive insistence upon its rights as a neutral, in case the members of the League applied sanctions against a Covenant-breaking state.

In the following year, when the Conference was engaged in drawing up the actual terms of a disarmament convention, Mr. Davis, on the authority of the President of the United States, reiterated that the United States was willing to consult, as part of its policy, which was "to co-operate . . . to secure a general disarmament agreement." The American offer was, in fact, in the words of the authority just quoted, "contingent upon the conclusion of a Disarmament Convention," and he sums up the position by remarking: "At London, the United States refused to give a pledge of consultation as a *quid-pro-quo* for French disarmament; at Geneva, the United States demanded general disarmament as a *quid-pro-quo* for a pledge of consultation. The shift in initiative gave the United States a considerable strategic advantage."

IN the discussions in the European Assembly at Strasbourg a school of thought has emerged which has come to be described as "functionalism." What those who use this term mean by it is that there is a way of looking at world affairs not in terms of countries but of "functions," or, to use a simpler expression, occupations. If you bring men together as nationals, so the argument runs, as Frenchmen, Italians, Germans and so on, divergent interests will very soon make their appearance. But if you assemble them in terms of their occupations, the deeper they get into the heart of their subject the more conscious they will become of the bond that unites them, whether they are doctors or chemists, or bankers, or electricians or astronomers.

Those who talk in this way sometimes go on to say that they have discovered a new approach to European unity, or even to world unity—*unity by functional association.* This is of course an exaggerated claim. What they have really done is to use an old approach which can be helpful, as they think, in a new setting, the setting of postwar Europe, where it can be effective in circumventing certain temporary political obstacles. The new Coal and Steel Authority is a case in point. Whether this authority will fulfill the hopes of its creators is not a matter for discussion in these pages. The point for us to note here is that, insofar as it succeeds in doing so, it will be because its operations are carried on *in a favorable political atmosphere.* Functional organizations cannot solve political problems. The most that they can do is to help to develop conditions in which political problems can be solved elsewhere, by statesmen, whose task it is *to grapple with questions of power.* It is a dangerous illusion to believe that functionalism by itself can bring about world peace, however fully it is developed. No conceivable multiplication of professional or workers' organizations can do away with the world's need for *political* organization; for it is only when men meet as *citizens,* taking responsibility for all the separate needs and interests in their community—whether on the local, national, or world-wide level—that they are really facing the issues of peace and war which, as has just been said, are issues of *power*.

Functional organizations are therefore not at the center of the problem of world peace; they do not minister directly to its main objective or provide it with its chief driving power. They are, so to speak, on the side lines, a sort of external appendage. And this is, in fact, the role that they have played in the League of Nations, and are playing today in the United Nations, where they are correctly, if uninspiringly, described as Specialized Agencies.

Nevertheless, the importance of these functional agencies or World Services of the United Nations, as they might be more fitly called, should not be made light of just because it has been overestimated in the past. During the period that we have been considering, the period of expedients, it was natural to turn to them as a sort of consolation prize for the failure of the League of Nations in its main task. Moreover, at that time, particularly in the very first years of the League, in the early twenties, progress in this field was swift and easy, because the mere fact of the creation of the over-all international secretariat made it possible to bring together and co-ordinate the various existing functional agencies, some of them going back to the eighteen-sixties. The establishment of the United Nations with the United States as a leading member has brought about another burst of activity in this field.

WORLD WAR II

SECTION VII

WORLD WAR II

"Westward look, the land is bright!"

CHAPTER 46: *The Finest Hour*

AT the opening of the first volume of his *History of the Second World War* Mr. Winston Churchill placed these words: "How the English-speaking peoples, through their unwisdom, carelessness and good nature, allowed the wicked to rearm."

After briefly recounting this story in the case of the United States, it must now be taken up even more briefly in relation to Great Britain: for in this case the consequences of the "unwisdom, carelessness and good nature" have been more lasting and have an important bearing on her present condition in the world and on her place in the United Nations.

Like other nations, Great Britain made many mistakes in her foreign policy in the interwar period and future British historians may be trusted not to gloss them over. What can be said in fairness is that, broadly speaking, they were not due to love of power or any other form of national selfishness on the part of the British people but simply to bad judgment resulting from congenital aloofness toward outsiders. Before 1914, so far as world affairs were concerned, Britain—and in this connection the term includes the self-governing Dominions—was not a full democracy. She was an aristocracy, and external affairs, remote from the experience of the great bulk of the people—that experience which is the chief justification of government by the common man—were in the hands of a small governing class. Effective power was divided between a few members of the Cabinet always including the prime minister and the foreign secretary, the foreign office—entry into which was at that time still obtained through rigid tests drawn up on a class basis—and a mere handful of members of the House of Commons who happened to take an interest in the subject. World War I and Woodrow Wilson's public addresses between them brought home to the British people the vital importance of world affairs and their bearing on their own individual lives. But in the existing state of public knowledge the first effect of this—and it lasted throughout practically the whole of the interwar period—was disastrous. The British voter, so experienced in domestic and civic affairs, needed to be brought up sharply against the hard test of reality before he learned his bearings in world affairs, and the process has been very costly. But in all his excursions into foreign affairs, at least so far as major issues were concerned, he acted for the best—even when he was unwittingly paving the road to misfortune.

These reflections suggest a question which has an important bearing on our subject and on the organization of the United Nations. If the British people, the leader of the world in the nineteenth century, with all its experience in trade, finance, and other forms of world intercourse, proved unable to adjust the management of foreign policy to the existing forms of parliamentary and democratic government, what about the other seventy or more states of the world, whose peoples, are all of them, under mid-twentieth century conditions, vitally interested in world affairs and in their effective management?

On September 2, 1939, Mr. Arthur Greenwood, a blunt and sturdy Yorkshireman, spoke out roughly in the House of Commons protesting against the slowness of the government in honoring the British guarantee to Poland. His was the authentic voice of British democracy. But he spoke twenty years too late. Must leadership among the free peoples always be twenty years—or twenty months or twenty days or even twenty hours too late?

The most calamitous of the British mistakes of judgment was the failure to intervene, and the pressure brought upon France not to intervene, when Hitler reoccupied the Rhineland in 1936. This single act, in which not a shot was fired, reversed the balance of power in Europe and set Hitler free to resort to aggression, East or West, at his own time. He was not slow to use this opportunity. In 1937, he secured control over Austria. In 1938, he imposed his will on Czecho-Slovakia, sealing his victory in his Munich Agreement with Great Britain, France, and Italy. In 1939, being now in a position to attack that country from the South as well as from the West, he sent his armies into Poland.

British opinion, at length awakened to realities, reacted strongly and at the end of forty-eight hours Britain and France were at war.

The German armies overran Poland with ease. When this had been accomplished, Hitler paused to make an offer of peace on the basis of his success in the East. He was genuinely surprised when the British government and people would hear nothing of it. As Mr. Churchill puts it:

> He felt sure that a peace offer would enable Mr. Chamberlain and his old colleagues, having vindicated their honour by declaration of war, to get out of the scrape into which they had been forced by the warmongering elements in Parliament. It never occurred to him for a moment that Mr. Chamberlain and the rest of the British Empire and Commonwealth of Nations now meant to have his blood or perish in the attempt.

Thus hostilities went on, with little more than patrol actions in the West. This "twilight war" continued until the following April, when it was sharply broken by the German occupation of Denmark and descent upon Norway. This caused a severe shock in Britain, involving as it did, a blow to the Navy, and it led almost immediately to the resignation of the Chamberlain government and the formation of an administration headed by Mr. Winston Churchill; this remained in power until July, 1945, after the end of the German war.

In May came the attack in the West—on Holland, Belgium, and France—with the break-through in the Ardennes, the rolling up of the allied armies and the improvised evacuation of the British and some French troops from the beaches of Dunkirk, carried out partly in the pleasure boats of private citizens. The British returned cheering and with no sense of defeat; "the others may be knocked out, but we have got into the finals," was their prevailing sentiment. But they had had to leave all but their rifles on the beaches. On June 22 came the armistice involving the suspension of all hostilities in metropolitan France.

During the eighteen months that followed—the period between Dunkirk and Pearl Harbor—the British Commonwealth fought on alone against all the strategic probabilities, at least as the experts elsewhere saw them. This experience has left an enduring imprint on the British mind and should never be forgotten by those in charge of the foreign relations of the United States. If Hitler had secured control of the Atlantic by a British capitulation in 1940, the agglomeration of power in the Old World would have placed the smaller island in immediate peril. Englishmen during those exhilarating months of the Battle of Britain and the blitz did not allow such thoughts to rise to the surface of their minds; but there are some might-have-beens which, in their psychological bearings, form part of the stuff of history.

CHAPTER 47: *The Combined Chiefs of Staff*

WHEN Hitler failed in his first attempt upon Britain, he broke off the engagement for the time being and decided to free his hand in the East before renewing the assault. In June, 1941, he launched an attack on the Soviet Union, which carried his armies to the outer edge of the oil deposits in the Caucasus before they were forced to retreat in January, 1943, after a portion of the German forces had been encircled at Stalingrad.

It was part of Hitler's global plan that Japan should join in the attack upon the Soviet Union by military and naval action in the Middle East. A Tripartite Pact between Germany, Italy, and Japan had been signed in Berlin on September 27, 1940, but this was couched in terms so vague as to allow the Japanese the full right of interpreting any given situation. In March, 1941, Matsuoka, the Japanese Foreign Secretary, visited Berlin, where Hitler and Ribbentrop made strenuous efforts to win Japan over to the German side, arguing that it was "now only a question of time until England would admit having lost the war." Matsuoka replied that, on the whole, he personally agreed with Hitler's view, but that "there were in Japan, as in other countries, certain intellectual circles which only a powerful individual could hold firmly under control. Japan would take action in a decisive form if she had the feeling that otherwise she would lose a chance which could only occur once in a thousand years." He went on to tell Hitler of the conference that he had had with Stalin on passing through Moscow on his way to Berlin. He had told Stalin that the Anglo-Saxons represented the greatest hindrance to the establishment of the New Order and that they were the common foe of Germany, Japan, and Soviet Russia. After some reflection, Stalin had said that "Soviet Russia had never got along well with Great Britain and never would." However, in spite of the confidence which the Japanese emissary showed in revealing these conversations to his German host, Hitler did not respond by disclosing to him his own intention to attack the Soviet Union within a few months' time.

When Matsuoka returned to Japan at the end of April, he found that the wind had changed in his absence and that the Cabinet had been considering the possibilities of an understanding in the Pacific with the United States. Thus, when, in the middle of June, Hitler declared war on the Soviet Union, Japan remained neutral and Matsuoka, who had "lost face" because he had not known of Hitler's intentions, resigned from office a few weeks later.

Thus it was that the Germans and the Japanese came to be out of step. The Japanese decision not to "lose a chance which could only occur once in a thousand years" was delayed for another six months and, when it came, it was as great a surprise to Hitler as it was to Washington. However, immediately on hearing of it, Hitler gave the German navy orders to attack American ships wherever found, and thus within a few days the United States was at war with Germany as well as with Japan.

Such is international co-operation when it is carried on between confederates each bent only on his own advantage without any common principle and purpose or any common ethical standard to sustain it.

Very different was the partnership between those whom Stalin called "the Anglo-Saxons." During the second phase of World War II, through the campaigns that were planned and carried on in the West and in the East, the teamwork on the higher levels was a model of what can be achieved by skilled organization when it is applied with selfless devotion to a cause transcending the particular interests of the partners.

This result was brought about, first, by the character and influence of the chief personalities concerned, without which the necessary confidence could never have been engendered and, secondly, by bringing to bear upon the conduct of the global war the experience of the art of public administration in its broadest scope and most up-to-date development.

This teamwork was maintained, first of all by constant communication on the highest level between the President of the United States and the British Prime Minister, confirmed and refreshed by face to face meetings whenever these were considered necessary: and, further, by a regular organization that was set on foot to execute their decisions.

This organization, which had its seat in Washington, was that of the *Combined Chiefs of Staff*—that is to say, of the chiefs of the army, navy, and air force of the United States and Great Britain. It was these six men who, acting on the instructions of their associated political chiefs, were responsible for the conduct of the war by land, sea and air, without a single false note amid all the complexities of logistics, until the victory of the free peoples was gained.

The story is told for the general reader in the report submitted to the American government, and to the world, by the Chief of Staff of the United States Army at the close of the war. As one reads General Marshall's concise and comprehensive record of simultaneous movement in six different "theaters of operation," one should pay the fighting men the recognition of trying to realize, however imperfectly, the nature and extent of the effort concealed between the simply written lines.

The Combined Chiefs of Staff organization is an important milestone on the road to world peace. Its technical details are no part of our subject. But something must be said about its spirit; for it was a perfect example of the mutual confidence, respect, and friendship without which no enduring structure of world peace can be built up. For a civilized world needs above all not blue prints, but men.

Only a few incidents, revealing the spirit of the Combined Chiefs of Staff, can be recorded here. When General Marshall took leave of his post after the victory, his three British colleagues, in bidding farewell to one who had "earned" their "personal affection as well as their professional respect", addressed to him a tribute which included these words: "Throughout your association with us in the higher direction of the armed forces of America and Britain, your unfailing wisdom, high principle, and breadth of view have commanded the deep respect and admiration of us all. Always you have honored us by your frankness, charmed us by your courtesy and inspired us by your singleness of purpose and your selfless devotion to our common cause."

When Field Marshal Sir John Dill, head of the British Joint Staff Mission in the United States, died in Washington of pernicious anemia in November, 1944, he left a request with his wife that he be buried in Arlington Cemetery, as he considered his work in the United States the most important in his life. Lady Dill asked General Marshall to read the Lesson at the burial.

In honor of the services rendered by Sir John Dill, the United States Senate passed a Joint Resolution paying tribute to his "outstanding service to the United Nations," an unprecedented action on the part of that body.

CHAPTER 48: *Hiroshima*

ON July 16, 1945, two months after the end of the Allied campaign against Germany and while a conference of the victorious Powers was in session at Potsdam, an atomic bomb was successfully exploded in a trial experiment in New Mexico.

This was the culmination of work which had been carried on since the latter part of 1941 under government auspices both in the United States and Great Britain. In the latter country, Mr. Winston Churchill authorized on August 30, 1941, that action should be taken under the direct supervision of a Cabinet Minister, Sir John Anderson. A very little later, "in the fall of 1941," President Roosevelt appointed a committee consisting of Colonel Stimson, as Secretary for War, Vice-President Wallace, General Marshall, Dr. Vannevar Bush, and Dr. James B. Conant to advise him "on questions of policy relating to nuclear fission."

A frank and well-documented account of the developments which followed, so far as the United States was concerned, is given in Stimson's autobiography.

The policy of the President and his advisers was a simple one. It was to produce an atomic weapon at the earliest possible moment. The reason behind this policy was equally simple—

namely, that it was known that the Germans were conducting similar experiments. They were indeed believed to be ahead of the Allies in this matter, since the original achievement of atomic fission had occurred in Germany in 1938. There was also a further motive, quite apart from the question of German competition. From the beginning it was realized by Stimson and his associates that a great new weapon of this kind might result in "shortening the war and minimizing destruction."

When the New Mexico trial "measured up to" the "highest estimates" of the scientists, it was at once realized that there was a good chance of insuring these latter aims.

At that time the United States forces, after their successful campaigns over the Pacific and on Okinawa, were preparing for a landing in Japan.

It was estimated that this operation would not be concluded until the latter part of 1946, at the earliest, and that it might be expected to cost over a million casualties to American forces alone. Judging by previous experience, enemy casualties would be much larger than this. The total strength of the Japanese army in July, 1945, was estimated at about five million men, which later proved to be very close to the official Japanese figures. The Japanese Army was in much better condition than the Navy and Air Force, which had borne the main brunt of the war.

In view of these facts, it was decided that a solemn warning should be addressed to the Japanese from Potsdam by the chief representatives of the United States, Great Britain, and China, calling upon them to surrender in view of the "varied and overwhelming character of the force" which was about to be brought to bear upon their islands. This warning, which included a "disavowal of any attempt to extirpate the Japanese as a race or to destroy them as a nation" and made no mention of the Emperor, thus indirectly implying that he would remain the source of authority, was duly delivered on July 26. On July 28 the Japanese Premier rejected it as "unworthy of public notice." On August 6 an atomic bomb was dropped by an American Army airplane on the city of Hiroshima and three days later, on August 9, a second bomb was dropped on Nagasaki. Of these two cities Hiroshima was an army center, being the headquarters of the Japanese Army defending Southern Japan and a major military storage and assembly point, while Nagasaki was a major seaport and contained several large industrial plants of great wartime importance. On August 10, after a prolonged Cabinet meeting, in which the deadlock was broken by the Emperor himself, the Japanese government decided to surrender and the war was over.

Seldom has a calculation been more completely justified. The two atomic bombs which were dropped were the only two which were ready and the rate of production at that time was very slow. But, in actual fact, it was not the bombs themselves which induced the Japanese to surrender. It was, as a leading scientist put it some months afterward, "the experience of what an atomic bomb will actually do to a community *plus the dread of many more.*" The air raid launched on Tokyo in March, 1945, by what have now, rather ironically, come to be known as "conventional" forces, caused far more casualties and damage than the atom bomb on Hiroshima.

Stimson's discussion of this subject concludes with an appraisal of the bearings of the discovery of atomic energy upon the foreign relations of the United States and upon the organization of world peace. As early as April, 1945, while the success of the New Mexico experiment was still in doubt, he had sent the President a memorandum concluding with these words: "If the problem of the proper use of this weapon can be solved, we would have the opportunity to bring the world into a pattern in which the peace of the world and our civilization can be saved."

Stimson hoped that the discovery of atomic energy, exercising a psychological effect on political *thinking* similar to that of the bomb on Hiroshima, might cause men to realize how worn out the old "pattern" was and so jolt them, by a sudden shock, into adopting a new one, a pattern of mutual confidence and co-operation. When he died in 1950, his immediate hopes had been disappointed, but his expectation that the new weapon would make the organization of world peace the most immediate and urgent business of mankind in the postwar period had been abundantly confirmed.

In the discussion of the United Nations, to which we now turn, the existence of the atomic weapon, with its vast potentialities for good or for evil, overshadows the whole argument. What began, centuries back, as a leisurely academic discussion and continued, at the Paris Peace Conference, at least in the eyes of the European statesmen, as a matter of secondary importance, has now become a question of the highest priority, demanding the attention of a Committee of Public Safety.

But how can such a committee be set on foot and who could keep it in order if it were?

PART II

The United Nations

The Lord shall give strength unto his people:
the Lord shall give his people the blessing of peace.

PSALM 29. 10

◇◇◇

THE WORLD AFTER WORLD WAR II

◇◇◇

SECTION VIII

THE WORLD AFTER WORLD WAR II

There are at present two great nations in the world. I allude to the Russians and the Americans. Both of them have grown up unnoticed and have suddenly assumed a most prominent place amongst the nations. . . . The principal instrument of the latter is freedom and of the former servitude.

— ALEXIS DE TOCQUEVILLE, in 1835.

CHAPTER 49: *The Equality of Peoples*

AT the end of World War II political conditions were very different from what they had been in 1939. The war that ended with the surrender of Japan had been a world war in the fullest sense of that term. It had shaken the whole of mankind; in particular, it had shaken regions that had previously been remote from the old European storm center: Australia and New Zealand, far away in the South Pacific and thought to be securely protected by British sea power; Africa, whose troops, under British leadership, had

153

taken part in the Burma campaign, bringing home many reflections from this excursion into the real Old World, and which, while the Mediterranean was closed and Egypt threatened, provided a highway for transport between the West and East and an alternative military base; and, above all, the most secluded and seemingly immovable region of all, Southern and Eastern Asia, home of more than half the population of the world. The Japanese conquest of Indo-China, Malaya, Burma, and Indonesia was indeed short-lived, but it was long enough to put an end to the inertia of centuries and to set flowing a fresh current of life among hitherto languid peoples.

That inertia, which some Western pseudo scientists had attributed to congenital racial inferiority and some armchair Western philosophers to a love of repose and a satisfying inner life, was largely due, as the West has now realized to its shame, to physical conditions. These can be remedied, once and for all, by means of the knowledge now available and by energetic action under Western leadership, so that, within a measurable period of time, the relative weakness of the nonwhite peoples, itself a fleeting occurrence in the long annals of mankind, will recede into history and true equality, in fact as well as in name, will prevail among the peoples. If, for some time to come, Asia is destined, as were Europe and even North America in their day, to pass through a tutelary period of preparation for full democracy, at least it will be under leaders of their own, holding up their heads as equals in the councils of the nations.

Nineteen forty-five will live in history, like 1848, as a year heralding the coming of freedom. But it is in the power of the peoples today, after a century of sad experience, to ensure that the consciousness of nationhood among the peoples of Asia will be accomplished without resistance by the overlords of yesterday and without conflicts on the part of the awakening nations among themselves.

CHAPTER 50: *The European Power Vacuum*

WORLD War I had cut down the number of the European Great Powers, the old arbiters of the destiny of the planet, from six to three—France, Italy, and Great Britain—while leaving Japan, a recent addition to their ranks, side by side with the United States. World War II completed this process. Britain emerged indeed with an enhanced reputation as a champion of freedom but greatly weakened, since she had been forced to draw upon her inherited financial resources and upon the narrow margin of her island strength. France, who had never recovered from the shock of 1870 and her great effort in World War I, had suffered war on her own soil for the second time in thirty years, this time with the added humiliation of a period of accommodation with the invader. Her social system, thanks to the abolition of privileges at the Revolution, was sounder than that of Great Britain and she had more natural resources to draw upon. Moreover, she was experiencing new vitality in the reversal of the previous long-continued decline of her birth rate and in her capacity to assimilate immigrants. Nevertheless her territorial limits, which had been so well fitted to the power scale of the old European system, were not adequate for an age when, if sovereign states wish to stand alone, they require defense in depth of a kind which France, like Great Britain, could never hope to provide. She, too, therefore could no longer be accounted a Great Power by the old scale of reckoning. Italy also was in much the same situation.

Thus in 1945, when the armies of the Western Allies and their Eastern partner converged on Central Germany, there was a vacuum of power in the old powerhouse of the world. It was filled, at least for the time being, by two non-European Powers, the United States and the Power whose rulers had adopted for it the name of "The Union of Soviet Socialist Republics" or, in more convenient language, the Soviet Union.

THE Soviet Union has not hitherto obtruded itself into these pages, except in the fleeting episode of its military excursion into China in 1929, because it is little concerned either with freedom or with order. It is, in fact, a negation both of freedom and of order, in the democratic and American sense of the latter word, as it is also, to use an expression which Gladstone once applied to another regime, a negation of God. But, at this stage of our inquiry, a short characterization of this strange political phenomenon would seem to be called for. It is not difficult to furnish this, since, on the one hand, all tyrannies are, broadly speaking, alike, and, on the other, the world has had thirty-five years in which to observe the Soviet Union and should by now be in a position to form a considered judgment upon its nature and conduct.

The Soviet Union is the last surviving example of the ancient empires of the Old World. It is a despotism like that of the rulers of Assyria and Babylon, unmitigated by the Greek influence which moderated the exercise of irresponsible power in the case of the Romans. Insofar as the Soviet Union has roots in Europe, those roots are Byzantine rather than West European. Its rulers have shown great skill and ingenuity in adapting for their rigidly centralized administration the latest scientific inventions of the West. While America has been learning how to use these in order more effectively to *diffuse power*, Stalin and his confederates have employed them in reverse, in order to concentrate power more effectually in their own hands.

The rulers of the Soviet Union have shown equal ingenuity in providing their regime with a camouflage of Western political principles, in order to conceal its true nature from lovers of freedom throughout the world. This was rendered possible for them by the circumstances under which they achieved ascendancy in 1917. They assumed power in the name of the European Socialist

The World After World War II

Movement and in the place of the most backward and ill-governed of the Great Powers, the Russian Empire of the Romanoffs. Lenin and Trotsky, who seized the reins in October, 1917, were not indeed the immediate successors of the Czars. They came in on the heels of an immature democratic regime. This had been unable to maintain itself in the aftermath of the World War I and the Revolution of March, 1917, which together had left Russia utterly disorganized. Lenin and Trotsky were no doubt sincere believers in the theories and policies that they had imbibed as young revolutionists in late nineteenth-century Russia and had developed further during their life as conspirators and exiles. But they soon disappeared from the stage, the former after a lingering illness, following a wound from an assassin's bullet, and the latter in exile in Mexico, murdered at long range by his relentless rival. For the last quarter of a century that sinister personage, Joseph Vissarionovich Djugashvili, who adopted the name of Stalin, has held the controlling power throughout the vast territory, or so-called Republics, of the Soviet Union, exercising it in a double capacity, as Chairman of the Council of Ministers and as General Secretary of the Communist party.

We must pause at this point to observe that each of these two last words contains an untruth. Soviet "communism" bears no resemblance to the system of common ownership of property to which that name has been applied over the centuries, while "the party," as it functions in the Soviet Union, has nothing in common with the party system which has developed in the West as an indispensable adjunct in the working of the representative principle in constitutional countries. One of the deadliest weapons of the Soviet system has been the systematic perversion of language, especially as regards terms in the theory and practice of politics. This originated with Karl Marx, the author of the miscalled *Communist Manifesto* of 1848, who, by refusing to admit that Political Science was a study in its own right and seeing the whole realm of the social sciences in terms of a single discipline, economics (which, incidentally, he misconceived in its turn), gave a wrong twist to political thinking which has confused and—no other word is adequate—bedeviled the minds of generations of honest inquirers, especially on the European Continent, and delayed the advance of political studies at a time when they were never so much needed.

Stalin's reign, viewed in perspective and set in the form of a diagram, reveals itself as a succession of zigzags. He has twisted and turned, moved this way and that, used stratagems and subterfuges, rid himself of competitors, actual or potential, with a disregard for consistency—not to say principle—worthy of a close student of Machiavelli and Cesare Borgia.

We have already had occasion to note his fundamental dislike of Great Britain, a feeling which certainly extends also to the United States; he has never visited either country, if for no other reason than fear for his personal safety. Thus, when World War II broke out, he calculated that Hitler and the Western Powers would exhaust one another and that he would be the gainer by remaining neutral. Hitler's victories in 1940 took him by surprise and, when the German invasion of Russia followed, he had no option but to range himself on the side of the Western Powers. They, on their part, were ready to forget his checkered past and to offer him help from their superior resources which may well have turned the scale in the hard-fought campaign which ensued.

When hostilities ended, the Soviet government, though seriously strained by the German invasion, was still upright and thus in a position to profit by the vacuum of power in Europe. Since Stalin's use of camouflage had involved a very systematic watch over all comment upon the Soviet Union on the part of Western statesmen and the Western press and radio, the Western peoples emerged from the war with a very distorted view of that regime and it took them several years before they caught up with the reality.

CHAPTER 52: *Stalin's Crucial Decision*

IN the meantime, Stalin had made a momentous choice. It was open to him, after the end of World War II, to profit by the favorable disposition of the American people by adopting a policy of international co-operation and making the most of the American help which was available to him at that time. This would have enabled him to repair the appalling losses which his territories had sustained through the German invasion and to take the strain off the people of Russia, who were in dire need of consumers' goods —as indeed they had been throughout the course of the successive economic "plans" of the Soviet regime.

This course was urged upon him by Kalinin, the President of the Soviet Union, who regarded the speediest rehabilitation of the country as the best policy in the interest of security, since so long as it was weak there would be a constant temptation for the "capitalist" countries.

Such a program would not have conflicted with Stalin's own long-term projects or with the declared objects of the Soviet Union's policy. He had made similar concessions to expediency in the past and could easily have done so again and found a suitable doctrinal excuse. But at this point opposition came from the Commissar of Foreign Affairs, Molotov, who argued that, according to the Marxian philosophy of history, Western civilization, already severely shaken by the economic depression of the early thirties and World War II, was doomed to early destruction and that it would be a grievous mistake to co-operate with it and so help to prolong its existence, merely in order to hasten their own economic recovery by a short space. Within two years, he said, economic depression would engulf the United States and the capitalist system would be overwhelmed—a prophecy which was later revised to *four* years.

Molotov's view prevailed with Stalin and it was the certainty of an approaching economic crisis in the United States which explains Soviet policy after the close of World War II, up to and including the Soviet Union's refusal to participate in the Marshall Plan, from which it had so much to gain. In his book, *The Way of the Free,* Dr. Osusky has recorded, on the authority of one of his compatriots, how, when the Czecho-Slovak delegation went to to Moscow in July, 1947, to inquire whether they should accept the Marshall Plan, Stalin told them that it was a fraud and that "nothing would ever come of it, because America would be struck by economic depression in the nearest future and forced to retire from the world scene in order to lick her wounds." Pressed to specify after the interview what Stalin meant by "the nearest future," the Czecho-Slovak Premier said that "he had the impression that Stalin expected the crisis to occur in 1948 or thereabouts."

It was in this state of mind that Stalin determined to make the most of the immediate opportunities offered to him by the European vacuum in order to extend his power in the West and in the East.

In the West he was favored by the military developments of the closing phase of the war. Had the Western Powers succeeded in liberating Holland as well as France and Belgium before the end of the campaigning season of 1944, they would have been in a much more advantageous diplomatic position than that in which they actually found themselves in the Yalta Conference of February, 1945, when public opinion was still under the impression of the German counteroffensive in the Ardennes. Equally, they would have had a stronger hand if they had succeeded in using their position in Southern Italy in order to secure a foothold on the Eastern side of the Adriatic. This was ruled out for what were no doubt sound logistical reasons. But the result was that, when the West and the East met around the council table to plan the concluding campaign of the war and draw the armistice line, Stalin secured an apportionment of territory which must have exceeded his utmost previous expectations. The line was drawn from Stettin in the western Baltic to Trieste at the head of the

Adriatic, leaving behind it, behind what we have now learned to think of as an iron curtain, in Mr. Winston Churchill's words, "all the capitals of the ancient states of Central and Eastern Europe"—Warsaw, Berlin, Prague, Vienna, Budapest, Belgrade, Bucharest, and Sofia. Only Athens and Istanbul remained in the free world.

Thus when Stalin decided to make light of the "Declaration on Liberated Europe" to which he gave his signature at Yalta—a declaration including, as its key words, the "right" of all the European peoples "to choose the form of government under which they will live"—he found that, in the existing vacuum, spoils were ready to his hand and he lost no time in picking them up. Putting together the acquisitions made by agreement with Hitler in the fall of 1939 and the gains made in 1945 and the immediately following years, before American opinion was aroused, he placed under Soviet rule the following formerly independent states: Estonia, Latvia, Lithuania, Poland, Rumania, Bulgaria, Hungary, Albania and, last but not least, Czecho-Slovakia, together with about one-third of Germany. In addition, he was in 1952 still in military occupation of the Eastern part of Austria. Moreover, after an unprovoked war against Finland in 1939-40, he had secured the handing over of a key fortress, thereby undermining the independence of that country. He also for a time exercised control over the strategically-situated land of Yugoslavia, where a regime modeled on Soviet lines had installed itself in power; however, since the Yugoslavs had succeeded in driving out the German invaders through an army of their own and also had access to the Mediterranean, the new ruler was able to maintain his independence after the war and so to rid himself of the control of Moscow.

Even greater immediate successes were obtainable for Stalin in the East. At the Yalta Conference, as a reward for promising to enter into the Japanese War within three months of the surrender of Germany, which, as it turned out, made him a belligerent for exactly six days, he secured the reversal of the results of the Russo-Japanese War of 1904-5. This involved, in concrete terms, control over the through railroad and the two key ports of

Manchuria, control over Northern Korea and the cession of the islands to the North and the Northeast of Japan. His control over Manchuria and of the Japanese arms made available there enabled Stalin to thwart the plans of the Chinese government for regaining its rightful possession of that province and enabled him also to give help to a group of Chinese confederates who had for several years already been in arms against the Chinese authorities. The United States made strenuous attempts to compose what seemed to many in the West at that time to be an internal quarrel. But these efforts proved unavailing, for reasons which only became clear after the event. Ultimately, in 1948, the satellites of Moscow, after having undermined the structure of the Chinese government, weakened by a decade of war, swept through the country and the Chinese authorities were forced to take refuge in the island of Formosa, access to which was barred to their opponents by the fleet of the United States.

Thus the power based upon the Heartland had extended its dominion over about 750 millions of human beings in the Old World, from the river Elbe in the West to the Southern borders of China in the East.

CHAPTER 53: *The Truman-Attlee-King Declaration*

THE successful use of Atomic energy, in the shape of two bombs, in bringing World War II to a close, brought about a general realization that the art of war had undergone a far-reaching transformation. It was clear that a source of power had been tapped which was capable of causing destruction on a hitherto unimagined scale—to the extent of bringing civilization, as hitherto known, to an end. The conclusion seemed obvious. Civilized mankind must, as soon as possible, place this destroyer which had newly appeared under effective control.

This was the moral drawn by the English-speaking world, and it was not long before its most representative statesmen embodied it in a definite proposal. On November 15, 1945, President Truman, Mr. Clement Attlee, and Mr. Mackenzie King, the leaders of the three states which had worked together on the atomic bomb project during the war, issued a declaration to the world—a declaration of which it has been said that "history will not disclose action by any government comparable to this generous offer." It proposed that, for the purpose of eliminating the use of atomic energy for destructive purposes and promoting its widest use for industrial and humanitarian purposes, "a commission should be set up by the United Nations. This commission should make proposals for the exchange of basic scientific information for peaceful ends, for the control of atomic energy to insure its use only for such ends, for the elimination from national armaments of atomic weapons and all the major weapons adaptable to mass destruction," and, finally, "for effective safeguards by way of inspection and other means to protect complying states against the hazards of violations and evasions."

In the following month the United States Secretary of State and the Foreign Ministers of Great Britain and the Soviet Union met in Moscow and agreed to the proposals for the setting up of a United Nations commission on atomic energy. On January, 1946, the newly established General Assembly of the United Nations approved the creation of the proposed atomic energy commission, giving it terms of reference which included the program outlined in the declaration of the three statesmen.

The key words in that declaration were the phrase *"effective safeguards by way of inspection and other means."* There is a long history behind those words. We have already seen that the pacifist program of disarmament proved unworkable in the thirties because its advocates had failed to think out their proposals to the full. Even if agreement had been reached on a *scale* of armaments, the conference of the thirties would have broken down on the problem of supervision over the execution of the agreed program. This was a matter which touched national susceptibilities to the quick. It was not easy to get naval and military men to accept the idea that "foreigners" should "pry around" their countries and scrutinize the way in which they were carrying out their disarmament obligations. For many years the United States government, while giving its support to the League of Nations policy of disarmament, continued to maintain that disarmament measures should be controlled on the spot—that is to say, by the various national authorities themselves. As the United States delegate to the Preparatory Disarmament Commission put it, on September 27, 1926, "any limitation of armaments must rest primarily upon international good faith and respect for treaties."

This was a typically American view, emanating from a country of "good neighbors." It did not carry conviction to the selfcentered and suspicious representatives of the Continental European states, especially when Hitler was upon the scene. Eventually, the United States government appreciated the force of the Continental European argument and reversed its position. On May 22, 1933, Mr. Norman Davis informed the Disarmament Conference at Geneva that the United States government believed that "a system of adequate supervision should be formulated to ensure the effective and faithful carrying out of any measure of disarmament" and that it was "prepared to assist in this formulation and to participate in the supervision." A few days later, on June 1, Mr. Davis declared that "adequate measures of supervision are an essential part of any effective system of disarmament" and that "*controlled disarmament is the safest road to peace.*"

These proposals led to no practical result, since Germany under Hitler was busy on an armaments program which was itself a treaty violation and she was naturally therefore not interested in armaments control by an international agency. However, the Soviet Union, which had taken part in the Geneva disarmament discussion ever since 1925, had long been on record in favor of the principle of international control. The Soviet proposal submitted to the Preparatory Commission on November 30, 1927, after outlining a very drastic program of "immediate, complete, and general disarmament" provided that "this program was to be controlled by a permanent international commission, with local commissions of control in every contracting state," and this was specifically worked out in the Soviet Draft Convention submitted to the plenary conference in 1932.

There seemed therefore, on paper at any rate, good reason to hope that the Soviet Union would co-operate in the policy set forth in the United States-British-Canadian Declaration.

Moreover, there were two good practical reasons to back up this hope. The first was that the Soviet Union had been taken completely by surprise by the success of the United States in the use of atomic energy and by the consequent change in the world balance of power. And the second was that the problem of control in itself had now become far less complex than that when it had been under discussion in the thirties; for what was involved then was to ensure that the agreed *scales* of armaments were adhered to, while what was now involved was a *total prohibition* of national action, so far as atomic energy was concerned.

It was not sufficiently realized in the West at that time that the whole of the Soviet action in Geneva, in which the pungent and cynical Litinov had been the leading spokesman, was an elaborate display of acting. The real position of the Soviet Union on the matter was stated with brutal frankness during the Sixth Congress of the Communist International in 1928, when an official speaker declared that "it goes without saying that not a single Communist thought for a moment that the imperialist world would accept the disarmament proposals."

It was therefore in a spirit of confidence and good will that the United States government set about making preparations for submission to the United Nations Commission.

But these proposals belong to the record of the United Nations and must be considered in their appropriate place.

PAVING THE WAY FOR THE

UNITED NATIONS

SECTION IX

PAVING THE WAY FOR THE UNITED NATIONS

"We were resolved to avoid the unhappy experience
of the League of Nations."

The Memoirs of Cordell Hull, p. 1653.

CHAPTER 54: *The Atlantic Charter*

IN following the evolution of the United Nations Charter, we
must begin by retracing our steps from the point reached in the
last section and carry our minds back to the second phase of World
War II—and indeed a little earlier.

Late in July, 1941, while the United States was still at peace and
Britain still under the threat of invasion and living under blitz and
antiblitz, President Roosevelt intimated to the British Prime-Min-
ister that "he would very much like to have a meeting with him in
some lonely bay or other." A week or two later, the two met on
shipboard in Placentia Bay in Newfoundland. They had many
practical matters to discuss together; but in both their minds there
was also a feeling that the time called for a common pronounce-

ment on the broad issues at stake in the war. It was the President who took the initiative when, in one of their first conversations, he said that "he thought it would be well" if they could "draw up a joint declaration laying down certain broad principles which should guide" their "policies along the same road." The Prime Minister lost no time in taking up the suggestion. The very next day he was ready with "a tentative outline of such a declaration."

The mimeographed copy of this document, with some corrections in ink by its author, is reproduced in his book and it is unnecessary to go into these details here. The Churchill document laid down five points, all of which may be described as being thoroughly Wilsonian. The two countries:

1. Seek no aggrandizement, territorial or other.
2. Desire to see no territorial changes that do not accord with the freely expressed wishes of the peoples concerned.
3. Respect the rights of all peoples to choose the form of government under which they will live. They are only concerned to defend the rights of freedom of speech and thought without which choice must be illusory.
4. Will strive to bring about a fair and equitable distribution of essential produce, not only within their own territorial boundaries but between the nations of the world.
5. Seek a peace which will not only cast down for ever the Nazi tyranny, but by effective international organization will afford to all states and peoples the means of dwelling in security within their own bounds and of traversing the seas and oceans without fear of lawless assault or the need of maintaining burdensome armaments.

The next day the President produced a revised draft which was taken as a basis of discussion. The chief difference from the Prime Minister's five points was in the fourth, where the President wished to insert the words "without discrimination and on equal terms." The Prime Minister insisted that, apart from any opinion of his own on the matter, he was not free to accept these words, since they might be held to contravene the Ottawa agreements for preferential trade and therefore the Dominion governments needed to be consulted. He also wished the word "markets" in the President's draft to be replaced by "trade."

The President, says Mr. Churchill in his account, "was obviously impressed and never raised the subject again." However, as we have already seen, Britain agreed to abandon the preferences and discriminations in question in the Lend-Lease Agreement of the following year. It is worth while remarking at this point that Secretary of State Hull was not present at the Atlantic Conference, as he was sick at that time. The State Department was represented by Mr. Sumner Welles, who prepared the President's draft.

Apart from the divergences already mentioned, the President's draft expanded the Prime Minister's five points to eight. The three added points were as follows:

Point 5 in the final document:

> They desire to bring about the fullest collaboration between all nations in the economic field, with the object of securing, for all, improved labor standards, economic advancement, and social security.

This was, of course, acceptable to the Prime Minister. It is to be noted that the United States was already at that time a member of the International Labor Organization.

Point 7 in the final document:

> Such a peace should enable all men to traverse the high seas and oceans without hindrance.

This took over part of the Prime Minister's original Point 5 with some change of wording, omitting the reference to armaments in that connection.

Point 8 in the final document:

> They believe that all nations in the world, for realistic as well as spiritual reasons, must come to the abandonment of the use of force. Since no future peace can be maintained if land, sea, or air armaments continue to be employed by nations which threaten, or may threaten, aggression outside of their frontiers, they believe that the disarmament of such nations is

essential. They will likewise aid and encourage all other practicable measures which will lighten, for peace-loving peoples, the crushing burden of armaments.

This, the Prime Minister at once remarked, omitted the reference in his own draft to an "effective international organization." He suggested the insertion of the words "pending the establishment of a wider and more permanent system of general security" before the reference to disarmament. This the President accepted.

The declaration was published on August 14 and soon came to be known as "The Atlantic Charter." It was well received in the United States, the principal criticism made against it being that, while it provided for three of the Four Freedoms, it made no mention of Freedom of Religion. This omission was soon rectified, as we shall see.

CHAPTER 55: *The Joint United Nations Declaration*

ON Sunday December 14, 1941, one week after Pearl Harbor and four months after the drafting of the Atlantic Charter, the Secretary of State asked one of his chief officials to "draw up a draft of a declaration to be made by the nations fighting the Axis, which would bind them together until victory and would commit them to the basic principles we uphold." Five days later the draft was sent to the President and three days after that Mr. Winston Churchill arrived in Washington. The President and he conferred together on the document, which was also shown to the Soviet and Chinese ambassadors. A slight change in the wording had been made to get over the difficulty that the Soviet Union was not at war with Japan. In accepting the document with minor amendments two days later, after it had been transmitted to Moscow, Mr. Litvinov made no objections, as it had been feared that he might, to the reference to religious freedom.

Thus it was that the Soviet Union became committed to the principles of the Atlantic Charter. For the Preamble of the Joint Declaration contains these words:

> Having subscribed to a common program of purposes and principles embodied in the Joint Declaration . . . known as the Atlantic Charter and being convinced that complete victory over their enemies is essential to defend life and liberty, independence and religious freedom, and to preserve human rights and justice in their own lands as well as in other lands . . .
>
> the Governments signatories hereto declare . . .

On the morning of December 31, when the text of the document was at last ready, the President came to the Prime Minister, as he was having a bath in the White House, and suggested to him that the Joint Declaration be entitled "Declaration by United Nations." "The distinguished bather," as the Secretary of State describes him in his account of the incident, agreed, "and thus the term UNITED NATIONS came into being."

When the document was ready, the question of arrangements for its signature had to be considered between the President and the Secretary of State. It was then that the President expressed the view that China and the U.S.S.R. should be taken out of the alphabetical order and put together with the United States and Great Britain at the head of the list. This was the origin of the distinction made later between the permanent and the elected members of the Security Council of the United Nations.

On January 2, the declaration, having first been signed, as the President had suggested, on behalf of the United States, Great Britain, the Soviet Union and China, was sent to the State Department for signature by the twenty-two other nations engaged in the struggle. All of them signed it the same day, "some of them," records Mr. Hull, "with obvious emotion." Between January 2,

1942, and March 1, 1945, there were twenty-one further signatories, making forty-seven in all.

The declaration contained two clauses. In the first the governments pledged themselves to employ their "full resources, military and economic" against the enemy. In the second, they pledged themselves to co-operate with one another and "not to make a separate armistice or peace." These, in the view of the Secretary of State, were necessary precautions against the recurrence of what happened in World War I, when the existence of secret engagements between individual allies had proved a serious complication in the negotiation of peace. The states which subscribed to the declaration were specially asked by the Secretary of State whether any such secret agreements existed and they gave him the assurance "that there were no such agreements."

As a result, the United States could this time enter the war not as an "associated power" but as a full ally.

The fact that the signature of France was absent from the declaration, since the Free French had not received recognition from the United States, led to a discussion amongst the President and his advisers as to the possibility of allowing adhesion to the document by "political groups representative of the peoples of countries overrun by the Axis which had no governments functioning in exile." Such adhesions could not, of course, rank on the same level as governmental signatures; nevertheless their representative quality might give them a certain value. A statement was therefore issued saying that the United States government, as the depository for the declaration, was ready to receive "statements of adherence to its principles from appropriate authorities which are not governments." The results of this experiment were not happy. The Free French did not make use of the offer, but a flood of other adherences came in "from committees allegedly representing the peoples of a dozen other countries," many of which "were at odds with one another." "Several of our Allies," records Cordell Hull, "Russia in particular, objected to some of these groups"; altogether, he concluded, "the statement brought little but trouble."

This incident is worth recording because it illustrates the difficulty of following the advice of those who urge that "the people," as contrasted with their authorized representatives, should be given a certain responsibility in the conduct of international affairs. A more clearly defined form of association was later devised with the same object in view.

CHAPTER 56:   *The Connally and Fulbright Resolutions*

THE Atlantic Charter had put the question of a future world organization to maintain security distinctly in the background. The Secretary of State, however, was determined not to let this matter lie dormant. In July, 1942, in a speech largely devoted to postwar considerations, he "came out flatly in favor of the establishment of an international security organization," with the United States as a member, and declared that the United States should be able to use force, under its auspices, to maintain peace.

During the following year, he devoted much time and effort to winning support in Congress for this cause. He kept in close contact with leading members of both parties and, as he records, "seldom lost an opportunity to hammer home again and again to Senators and Representatives, whether Democratic or Republican . . . that a world organization to maintain the peace, by force if necessary, was absolutely imperative, and the United States had to be one of its principal members . . . and that United States policy in this respect should be entirely nonpartisan with both Republicans and Democrats joining in its support." As a result of his efforts, carried on with extreme care so as to avoid stirring the embers of past controversies, the House, on September 21, adopted a resolution, proposed by Representative Fulbright of Arkansas, "favoring the creation of appropriate international machinery with

175

power adequate to establish and to maintain a just and lasting peace among the nations of the world, and as favoring participation by the United States therein."

On November 5, on the proposal of Senator Connally of Texas, the Senate followed suit. The Connally resolution was to the effect that "the United States, acting through its constitutional processes, join with free and sovereign nations in the establishment and maintenance of an international authority with power to prevent aggression and to preserve the peace of the world."

The news of this event reached the Secretary of State as he was on his way home from a conference at Moscow to which we must now turn our attention.

CHAPTER 57: *The Moscow Conference*

DURING this period of the war President Roosevelt made several unsuccessful attempts to bring about a meeting with Stalin. The last of these had been in connection with the Quebec Conference in August, 1943. At about that time, however, the idea was put forward suddenly in the Soviet press that, though the Generalissimo might be preoccupied with the direction of the war, a meeting of the foreign ministers could well be held. The President and the Prime Minister both took up this suggestion and on August 24 Stalin agreed to it.

Anxious to spare the Secretary of State the fatigue of a long journey, the President offered the Soviet authorities a number of alternative meeting places. Stalin, however, insisted on Moscow, and the Secretary of State told the President that, "wherever the conference might be held—anywhere between Washington and Chungking"—he "would be there" himself.

Cordell Hull was at that time nearly seventy-two. He had not lately been in good health and he had never before traveled by air. But he felt it his duty to fly to "the diplomatic engagement at

176

Moscow just as an officer has to take his unit into battle whether he wants to or not."

The conference in Moscow covered a wide range of topics, both as regards the conduct of the war and postwar arrangements. Cordell Hull, however, stuck firmly to the subject which was foremost in his mind—to secure the adhesion of the Soviet Union and China to a declaration favoring the establishment of an international organization. When he arrived in Moscow, he found that this subject had not been included in the agenda. He at once insisted that it be inserted and be made Point Two on the list, to which Molotov and, of course, Mr. Eden agreed.

When Point Two was reached, which was at the third meeting on October 21, Molotov said that "his government was very favorably disposed toward the principles set forth in the declaration and therefore welcomed it"; but he went on at once to raise an objection about China, saying that it would probably be impossible to secure her adhesion in time to sign the declaration during the conference. This led to an inconclusive discussion. During the recess that followed, Cordell Hull "took up very earnestly with Molotov his objections to including China in the declaration," arguing that American opinion would be "hopelessly rent" by the news that "the United States had joined with the Soviet government to throw China out of the war picture" and that this might lead to readjustments in American arrangements for carrying on the war. Immediately after the conference resumed, Molotov said that he was willing to leave open the question of Chinese participation.

The Secretary of State, however, was determined to put up with no delay. Working both through the Chinese Ambassador in Moscow and through the State Department by means of the United States Ambassador in Chungking, he succeeded in getting the wheels moving with the necessary speed. By the time of the last session of the conference, the Chinese Ambassador had received the full powers necessary to enable him to sign what thus became *The Four Nations Declaration on General Security* of October 30, 1943.

The preamble of the declaration recalls the terms of the United Nations Declaration of January 1, 1942. The most important clause of the declaration itself stated that the Four Nations:

> Recognize the necessity of establishing at the earliest practicable date a general international organization, based on the principle of the sovereign equality of all peace-loving states, and open to membership by all such states, large and small, for the maintenance of international peace and security.

In presenting the results of the conference to the Senate on November 18, the Secretary of State declared:

> As the provisions of the Four Nation declaration are carried into effect, there will no longer be need for spheres of interest, for alliances, for balance of power, or any other of the special arrangements through which, in the unhappy past, the nations strove to safeguard their security or to promote their interests.

Immediately after his return from Moscow, Cordell Hull intensified the planning work which had already been going on in the State Department for postwar international organization. A Division of Special Research on Postwar Problems had been created inside the department in February, 1941. This was followed within a few weeks of Pearl Harbor by the setting up of an Advisory Committee on Postwar Foreign Policy. This consisted of fourteen persons of whom seven, including the Secretary of State (who was Chairman), were in the department and seven were distinguished outsiders.

On December 29, some six weeks after his return from Moscow, the Secretary of State sent the President a memorandum representing the "latest ideas" of the Department of State team on postwar international organization. This was approved by the President on February 3, 1944, and the Secretary was authorized to go ahead with his planning on the basis of the memorandum, practically all the points in which were embodied in the United States proposals at the Dumbarton Oaks conference in the following August.

THE AMERICAN ROAD

SECTION X

THE AMERICAN ROAD

"The peoples who have experienced the benefits of a good constitution of their own are those best qualified to take the lead in the constant improvement of the broader constitution needed to ensure World Peace."

"An understanding of the United States is the best insurance for peace."

CHAPTER 58: *An Attainable Objective*

THE object of this book is to trace the American road to world peace. This goal, as the writer believes, can be reached by means of a constitutional document, the United Nations Charter, and in no other way discernible to the political thinker in the present age. That document, as it emerged from the conference which adopted it, embodied the consent of fifty nations, now increased to sixty. It contains provisions to ensure that its observance will be backed up, where necessary, by the use of force. Thus it aims at bringing about, and establishing once and for all in the life of humankind, that organic association between law and power of which so many political thinkers have dreamed in the past.

181

Such an association has been firmly established in the minds and hearts of the people of the United States by means of their own Constitution, which was also once a mere document. The framers of that document were wise, experienced and farsighted men and their work has proved effective and fruitful much beyond the hopes of most of their contemporaries. In dealing with the United Nations Charter, the men and women of sixty nations have the wisdom and experience of the whole world, past as well as present, to draw upon. It is therefore not wishful thinking but an expression of sober, considered judgment to declare that the problem of assuring world peace under conditions of freedom and justice by means of a constitutional document is as attainable today, through the wise exercise of the science and art of politics, as the forming of a more perfect union, the establishment of justice, the promotion of the general welfare, and the securing of the blessings of liberty has proved to be for the people of the United States of America.

CHAPTER 59: *The Two Principal Obstacles*

WE have now reached a point in this record when we are drawing very close to our objective. That objective is the establishment of an organization to secure world peace. Such an organization seemed to be within the reach of the civilized world a third of a century ago, when Woodrow Wilson conceived the design of the League of Nations. But his effort failed because the world, and particularly the American people to whom he appealed to take the lead, was not prepared for it. Today the situation is transformed. There is a mood of readiness on both sides of the Atlantic, and even across the Pacific.

Yet there is still the danger of a second failure through an insufficient understanding of the nature of the task. This task is difficult, but it is only the cowardly and the cynical who hold it to be impossible; for through the movement of events in recent years, particularly since 1945, it has become far more manageable than it was when Woodrow Wilson grappled with it. Today, we can see how it can be achieved in terms of political science; and, more than that, we can see how statesmen, equipped with the conclusions of political science and understanding how and when to make their appeal to the peoples, can bring such an organization into existence and enable it to function effectively.

Let us pause for a few moments on the threshold in order to face the chief difficulties that have to be overcome; for only if we are clear-sighted as well as determined can we hope to achieve our purpose.

Those difficulties have already been introduced to the reader at an early stage, so that they might serve as an undercurrent running through our story. Now the moment has come to recall them.

The first difficulty was that there seemed to be an inherent contradiction between the concept of democracy and the concept of large-scale political power. Democracy means government *by* the people, not simply government *of* and *for* the people. Its purest form is the New England town meeting, where those who exercise authority in the community meet their rulers, the citizens, face to face. Through the principle of representation the area of the democratic system was widened until it covered countries of the size of England or France. But this enlargement, as we have seen, though it enabled government by the people to function in regard to domestic affairs, never provided adequately for the democratic control of external or "foreign" affairs, lying beyond the experience of the immense majority of the citizen body. How then can we hope to extend the area still further until it covers the whole globe, or the territory of the sixty members of the United Nations, without sacrificing democracy in the process?

A way of dealing with this problem has now appeared which would have seemed fantastic to Greek and other pioneers of the democratic system.

The American Road to World Peace

It is the emergence of the United States of America as a single close-knit political community of over 150 million people—a community not only democratic in form but consisting of a population highly skilled in the technique of popular government, from the parish or precinct up to the federal level, and now accustomed to make use for this purpose of all the inventions of the physical scientists. This has made it possible for the United States to be a Great Power of a new kind, the first democratic power in the modern world and by far the greatest Power in the world. By the mere fact of its extension, in this close-knit form, over so vast an area, and through the cultural diversity of its citizen body, the American people has outgrown the parochial outlook which has hitherto been the limiting factor of democracy. It would be premature to claim that the American electorate in its present stage of education in world affairs has solved the difficulty of making large-scale power compatible with popular government. But at least it can be said that there is a growing realization, in many different sectors of the American community, of the existence and urgency of the problem and of the continuous effort needed for coping with it, if democracy is to survive. It can also be claimed that sufficient progress has been made to justify the confidence that, with the proper use of the facilities now available, the plain citizen can now acquire a broad world outlook qualifying him to form a judgment on external affairs with at least as much discernment and good sense as the more limited governing class of the older Great Powers.

How can such an outlook be brought about, diffused, and maintained? This is an educational problem which demands separate treatment. Let us do no more at this time than ask a question. Does an increase in *information* on world affairs automatically bring with it an increase of *understanding?*

We pass now to the second and even more insistent of the difficulties. Let us restate it.

The present-day world is in need of some kind of world authority, some authoritative guidance by statesmen who have the experience, the judgment, and the moral qualities needed for the exercise of such world leadership. But these statesmen must be real leaders, leaders in the democratic sense of the word, not just "superior persons" lifted above the level of the people and without any sense of relationship to them. Yet if they are to have this representative quality, if they are to be true world leaders, there must be some kind of community behind them toward which they feel their responsibility.

Such a community—let us admit it frankly—does not yet exist. The United States is a true political community—the largest in the world and one of the most genuinely democratic. And because it is a true political community, built up, bit by bit, through the extension of neighborhood relations from coast to coast, it is capable of indefinite expansion. Conceivably, it could extend throughout the globe, if the other peoples were willing to respond in the same spirit. That the other peoples are *potentially* ready, as individual men and women, to do so, is clear from the ease with which newcomers to the United States adapt themselves to the American way of life. Evidently, there is no contradiction in the nature of things between the American way and the world's way, insofar as the world as a whole *has* a "way." All over the world men and women *sense* that America represents something new and attractive which haunts them in contrast with their present condition.

But this widespread sense—the sense that lately caused an interruption of the traffic in a street in Eastern Europe because a shop there was exhibiting the catalogue of a well-known American mail order business—is not yet on the level of a public opinion. Still less is it the expression of an organic political community. Men have not yet learned to distinguish between *liberty* as a quality in their lives, as an integral part of their personality as human beings, and political *freedom* with its positive responsibilities in the realm of associated action. Till the individuals in the crowd in the East European street have made the effort which the relatives of many of them, who left to go overseas, made when they became American citizens, till they have become responsible citizens, members of a true political community, the right relationship between their country and the world authority cannot be established. In the meantime it will be little more than a formal or token relationship.

Thus our second difficulty admits of no easy solution. A true world authority based upon the participation of sixty or more nations is still, so far as practical statesmanship is concerned, a matter of time and effort. The political scientist can point out the road to it, for that road is clearly indicated. The process can be hastened by education; but it must be the right kind of education and, although there have been plenty of efforts made in the field called "education in world affairs," the kind needed to bring a world community into being has not yet been set on foot, in spite of the inexhaustible good will that has been shown in this endeavor, because it requires a type of effort different from any that has been yet undertaken, except on a very limited scale.

But this is a subject which calls for detailed examination in a later study.

Nevertheless even now we cannot acquiesce in a negative conclusion, for the problem that we have to face is an urgent one. It admits of no delay. The condition of the civilized world is very grave. There is a pressing need for remedial action, and it is the duty of every citizen, in the United States or elsewhere, who has the privilege of living under healthy political conditions, to address his or her mind to the claims of this need.

The need would exist quite apart from the discovery of atomic energy and the threat held over the free world by the refusal of the Soviet Union to join in placing this new instrument of destruction under an effective system of world control. The need is inherent in the interdependent conditions which have grown up in the last century or more following on the first period of scientific invention at the end of the eighteenth century. But the *urgency* of the need has been greatly intensified by the problem of atomic energy, which has raised in a sharp form the question whether there is room, in one and the same world, for uncontrolled atomic energy and the continuance of civilization as we have hitherto known it.

Let us therefore turn our attention next to the problem of atomic energy, leaving aside, for the moment, the outcome of Cordell Hull's preparations, as described in the foregoing section, in the Dumbarton Oaks and San Francisco conferences. For the problem of atomic energy, though it is closely related to the main theme of our inquiry, lends itself conveniently to separate treatment.

THE ATOMIC RECONNAISSANCE

SECTION XI

THE ATOMIC RECONNAISSANCE

"The true and legitimate goal of the Sciences is no other than
to benefit human life by new discoveries and resources."

— FRANCIS BACON, *Novum Organum*, Aphorism 81

CHAPTER 60: *The First Attempt to
Control Atomic Energy*

THE Truman-Attlee-King Declaration of November 15, 1945,
started a train of important political happenings in regard to
atomic energy. The first session of the newly-established Geneva
Assembly of the United Nations was due to meet in London in
January, 1946. It was preceded by a conference, held in Moscow
in December, of the Foreign Secretaries of the United States (former Supreme Court Justice James F. Byrnes had become Secretary of State on July 3, 1945), Great Britain, and the Soviet
Union.

Acting on the offer contained in the Truman-Attlee-King Declaration, the three Foreign Ministers agreed to recommend to the
General Assembly the establishment by the United Nations of a
commission "to consider problems arising from the discovery of
atomic energy and related matters." They also agreed to invite

the other two permanent members of the Security Council, France and China, together with Canada, to join with them in sponsoring a resolution of the General Assembly to that effect. A resolution establishing a United Nations Atomic Energy Commission was duly adopted by the Assembly on January 24, 1946. It was to be composed of one representative of each of the states represented on the Security Council, whether permanent or elected, together with Canada when she was not already sitting as an elected member. It was to submit its reports and recommendations to the Security Council and to receive directions from that body. This procedure was expressly laid down "in view of the Security Council's primary responsibility under the Charter of the United Nations for the maintenance of international peace and security."

Throughout these proceedings the Soviet government acted in concert with the United States and Britain, thus giving its approval to the principle of "effective safeguards" included in the Truman-Attlee-King Declaration. However, as Secretary Byrnes records, this result was not obtained without difficulty. The Secretary of State had proposed that the atomic energy resolution should be the first item on the Moscow Conference Agenda. Molotov took objection to this and proposed that it be put last. Mr. Byrnes agreed, thinking that the delay was needed in order that a distinguished Russian scientist, reported by the press to be in Paris, might have time to return to Moscow. This supposition, however, proved groundless, since, when the scientist in question eventually returned, he did not attend the conference. When the conference came to deal with its last item, Molotov proposed an innocent-looking amendment which would have had the effect of crippling the work of the commission. The Secretary then told him that, unless this was withdrawn, he himself would withdraw the entire resolution. Thereupon the Soviet Foreign Minister gave way and the atomic energy proposal "was agreed to with less debate than any other subject on the agenda."

Meanwhile in the United States a committee on atomic energy had been set up in the State Department, assisted by a board of consultants headed by Mr. David E. Lilienthal. The committee reported that the control of atomic energy by the United Nations, as proposed in the Truman-Attlee-King Declaration, could not be made effective unless there was an international system of enforcement. Such a system, in their opinion, would need to go beyond inspection and other methods of policing. Control was needed at every stage of the activity in dealing with the raw materials of atomic energy. Thus the only way to bring about effective control of atomic energy was to set up an organization with *positive* functions to deal with "all intrinsically dangerous nuclear operations."

On June 14 Mr. Bernard M. Baruch, who had been appointed the Representative of the United States on the Atomic Energy Commission, submitted a series of proposals based on the findings of the State Department committee. He began his speech with a forthright declaration attuned to the occasion: "We are here to make a choice between the quick and the dead." He then proceeded to propose the creation of an international atomic development authority which would be entrusted with the development and use of atomic energy at every stage, beginning with the raw material and extending through the manufacturing process right down to the finished product. The new authority would possess a large measure of autonomy and it would take its decisions, in the ordinary democratic manner, by majority vote. Mr. Baruch insisted that certain specific acts "such as the production and use of an atomic bomb, seizure of the authority's facilities, or any willful interference with the activities of the authority," should be "stigmatized as international crimes" and that "the appropriate punishment" should be "provided in the event of violation." All these proposals were to be embodied in a separate treaty, to which all nations would be invited to subscribe. Once the nations had adhered, no nation would be permitted to commit "any breach of the treaty without facing appropriate sanctions." As outlined to the Security Council, the proposed treaty, like the Kellogg Pact, would contain no provision for withdrawal. It would be "for ever and for ever."

On the all-important question of the punishment of those guilty of the crime of violating the treaty, Mr. Baruch's words were so weighty, and so specific, that they must be cited textually:

> It would be a deception to which I am unwilling to lend myself were I not to say to you, and to our people, that the matter of punishment lies at the heart of our present security system. It might as well be admitted, here and now, that the subject goes straight to the veto power contained in the Charter of the United Nations, so far as it relates to the field of atomic energy. The Charter permits penalization only by concurrence of each of the five great powers—the Union of Soviet Socialist Republics, the United Kingdom, China, France, and the United States. I want to make it very plain that I am concerned here with the veto power only as it affects this particular problem. There must be no veto to protect those who violate their solemn promise not to develop or use atomic energy for destructive purposes.

The rest of the story up to the present time can be quickly told. On June 19 the Soviet Union put forward a series of counterproposals in the form of a treaty prohibiting the production and use of atomic energy, but containing no provisions for inspection or supervision or any international machinery of control, beyond the Security Council operating under the existing system—that is to say, including the Great Power veto. To this position the Soviet Union adhered substantially through some 200 meetings of the Atomic Energy Commission and its various committees between June, 1946, and May 17, 1948; at that point the commission reported to the Security Council that it "had reached an impasse." This report was submitted to the General Assembly and led to a statement by Senator Warren Austin, the United States representative on the Security Council, in the course of which he made it quite clear, to any who might still be in doubt on the subject, that the United States was ready to abandon its own right of veto so far as the control of atomic energy was concerned. "In this matter," said the Senator, "the interest of the United States is no different from the interest of any other country. Any weakness in the plan of control which would allow the possibility of a new threat of atomic weapons anywhere in the world after the signing of the treaty would be disastrous to peace and security. There is no nation great or small which would be willing to envisage such a possibility."

The nature of the "impasse" referred to in the 1948 Report was spelled out in the following concluding paragraph of a statement made by the representatives of Canada, China, France, the United Kingdom, and the United States on October 25, 1949; these Powers had been requested by the General Assembly in November, 1948, "to hold consultations in order to determine whether there exists a basis for agreement on the international control of atomic energy. . . ." They reported:

> These consultations have not yet succeeded in bringing about agreement between the U.S.S.R. and the other five Powers, but they have served to clarify some of the points on which there is disagreement. It is apparent that there is a fundamental difference not only on methods but also on aims. All of the sponsoring Powers other than the U.S.S.R. put world security first and are prepared to accept innovations in traditional concepts of international cooperation, national sovereignty, and economic organization when these are necessary for security. The government of the U.S.S.R. puts its sovereignty first and is unwilling to accept measures which may impinge upon or interfere with its rigid exercise of unimpeded state sovereignty.
> If this fundamental difference could be overcome, other differences, which have hitherto seemed insurmountable, could be seen in true perspective, and reasonable ground could be found for their adjustment.

The American public had been prepared for this pessimistic conclusion for some time past; for already in January, 1948, Dr. J. Robert Oppenheimer, a distinguished physicist who was then Chairman of the Advisory Committee of the United States Atomic Energy Commission and who, as Director during the war, of the Atomic Bomb Project Laboratory at Los Alamos, New Mexico, had been the leader in the successful tests in July, 1945, had contributed an article to *Foreign Affairs* which read like a valedictory to the Baruch plan. Indeed, his conclusions were distinctly more pessimistic than those of the veteran legislator, Senator Austin; for he complained of "the lack of reality of all the discussions up to date." It should not be forgotten, he wrote, "that, were there more reality to the plans for the internationalization of atomic energy, we ourselves, and the governments of other countries as well, would have found many difficulties in reconciling particular national security, custom, and advantage with an over-all plan for insuring the security of the world's peoples"; "but these problems," he added, "had not arisen in any serious form."

The contrast between the positive attitude of Senator Austin with his readiness to align the United States with the other nations "great or small" in seeking to achieve peace and security and the mood of chastened resignation discernible in the article of Dr. Oppenheimer invites a few words of comment. Dr. Oppenheimer's attitude would seem to represent the reaction of a natural scientist who has, for the first time in his working life, been brought sharply up against the complexities of international politics. It is perhaps not going too far to describe his attitude as a rebound from the impatient idealism in which some of his professional colleagues indulged when the project of internationalization was first launched. These natural scientists realized, more quickly than the general public, the far-reaching implications of the Baruch Report. They saw that it involved—not indeed a world government but at any rate an *element of world government*. And they set themselves to popularize this concept, through such public-spirited enterprises as *The Bulletin of the Atomic Scientists* and in other ways. But when the walls of Jericho did not fall down at the blast of their trumpet, they were tempted to become discouraged. For they had had no training in political science; they lacked the background knowledge and the political "know-how" which can be felt behind the words of Senator Austin. Where Dr. Oppenheimer is passive and melancholy, Senator Austin, for whom, as befits an American in action, the word "impossible" does not exist.

is indignant. He is well aware of the nature of the "innovations in traditional concepts of international co-operation, national sovereignty, and economic organization" which are needed to give the American people, and all peoples, security. But he is not prepared to acquiesce tamely in Dr. Oppenheimer's conclusion that "it appears most doubtful if there are now any courses open to the United States which can give our people the sort of security they have known in the past." To talk in this way is to proclaim the bankruptcy of political science. Senator Austin knows that, at the rate at which the "traditional concepts" in international politics have been moving in recent years and months, the adjustments needed to give the world security are well within the capacity of experienced statesmanship and that the real obstacle is not in the realm of technique, but is simply *bad will*, bad will on the part of one individual, the master of the Politburo, the man at the apex of the Soviet pyramid of power. The Romans had an expression which is to the point in this connection. They stigmatized a particular kind of offender as "an enemy of the human race." That is exactly what Joseph Stalin and his associates are. They are criminals so hardened that when they are asked to choose between the continuance of their evil practices and the safety of the rest of mankind, they stubbornly stick to the former. If ever there was a case when the intervention of the law was called for, is it not here? That surely is the right reaction, the civilized man's reaction, to the position in which the world has been left by the Soviet refusal to co-operate in placing this new terrible power under effective control. And that was the reaction of the Secretary of State, a former Justice of the Supreme Court, when he recorded his experiences in dealing with his Soviet opposite number. "I deny," he says outright, "that the Charter of the United Nations . . . can be nullified by a single veto of a permanent member of the Security Council. . . . There are principles of law incorporated in the Charter which should be regarded as the law of all lands. These principles *will* be regarded as the law of all lands if we and all other members of the United Nations make it clear that we are determined, if need be, to defend them by force."

BEFORE we leave this subject, let us look at it briefly from a different angle, from the angle from which Stalin and his confederates were bound to regard it.

For them acceptance of the Baruch Report would have meant making a breach in the hitherto impenetrable wall of Soviet sovereignty—a breach, moreover, which could not be concealed from their own people, for it would have entailed the granting of permission to officials of the United Nations to travel throughout the length and breadth of the Soviet Union and to examine, without previous notice, any mine, factory, or other installation which they chose to visit.

During the period between 1945 and 1948, when the control of atomic energy was under active discussion, public attention was so much occupied with the debate between the Soviet Union and the Powers which accepted the Baruch Report that perhaps insufficient attention was paid to the full implications of the latter. These were seen very clearly then by some political scientists and it is necessary to go into them briefly here; for, as was pointed out at that time, the Baruch Report, through the new organization which it would necessarily bring into being, may well "yield the clue for solving the most intractable of all problems, the creation of some form of what, for want of a better name we call a World State."

These last words are taken from an essay contributed by three distinguished British political thinkers to a volume entitled *Atomic Energy; its International Implications* published in London in 1947. The essay in question only covers ten pages, but its pregnant paragraphs go to the heart of the matter. When political agreement has been reached "on the basic principle of control," they write, "it will be necessary to set up a directing, policy-making body to act in the name of the United Nations." This body, which, they suggest, might be called the Atomic Energy Agency, would need "a large executive staff of international servants to carry out its decisions on inspection, control, and development all over the world." The duties of this staff would be partly technical and partly administrative. On the technical side, "it should be possible to find sufficient men imbued with an international outlook" and "the unique opportunities for research are likely to attract highly skilled scientists." On the administrative side, the organization of an international staff charged with such responsible duties would involve very complex problems. For instance, "some officers may have to be entrusted with secrets of far-reaching significance. . . . The essential thing," they conclude, "is that the machine should win the confidence of the governments and peoples of the world, so that they believe that these great issues are in the hands of competent men of integrity."

There is no need to emphasize the delicate nature of the task proposed for these administrators, since this has been painfully illustrated by certain events which have occurred since the words just cited were written. In the unstable conditions of our time, when the effects of ultraspecialization are insufficiently counterbalanced by a broader educational approach and more enduring values, certain physical scientists entrusted with highly responsible tasks, men of brilliant attainments in their own fields, have been revealed as holding dangerously distorted views as to what constitutes "integrity." The influences which have brought about this strange psychological phenomenon are unhappily still active and potent. They will only be fully removed when the present conditions of stress and strain have themselves passed away and a climate of settled peace has supervened. Until that has come about, the task of setting up a body like the Atomic Energy Agency will, to say the least, not be a simple one. It has not proved simple in the case of national atomic organizations. It will be even more difficult in the case of an international organization in the same field.

Let us return now to an examination of the proposed agency as a directing and policy-making body. How large should it be?

"Experience has shown," say the three writers, "that eleven or twelve is the maximum for efficiency" in a body of this kind. Many years ago President Eliot of Harvard fixed on *seven* as the right number to discuss a complex matter of business, "because that number of men can sit around a small table, talk with each other informally without waste of words or any display of pretense, provide an adequate diversity of points of view and modes of dealing with the subject in hand, and be prompt and efficient in the discharge of business." Human nature does not change and a small round table keeps its fixed limits. The three distinguished writers visualize an organization constituted on the model of the Security Council and the Atomic Energy Commission; that is why they enlarge the optimum number of seven to eleven or twelve, in order to provide room for representatives of the five Great Powers and of at least six other states. But the comparison between the Atomic Energy Agency and the Security Council is misleading, because the members of the Security Council, like the members of the League of Nations Council before them, do not "sit around" a small table. They sit on one side of a long curved table, shaped rather like a wide horseshoe, a position which makes it difficult for them to "talk with each other informally."

Moreover, the members of the Security Council and of the Atomic Energy Commission are representatives of their respective states. Should the members of the proposed agency be representatives or should they be appointed in their individual capacity? On this very important question the three writers refrain from expressing a definite opinion. They confine themselves to saying that "some may think that they (the members of the agency) should have permanent tenure and, therefore, be appointed in their individual capacity," adding that the agency as a whole "must be representative of the whole body of states." As there are sixty states in the United Nations, these words cannot mean that each individual state will be represented in the agency. It is clear then that the writers are using the word "representative" in a broad sense, meaning that the persons chosen must be of a stature or quality enabling them to be regarded as representative world figures; they must, if we may adapt a phrase current in American politics, be of international "timber." If that is the object aimed at, does not this automatically rule out the idea that the members of the agency should be appointees of individual governments? Should they not, as world figures, be appointed by some body which itself represents the world or a large section of it, such as the General Assembly of the United Nations or a Regional Council?

We can do no more now than to raise these questions: but it will already have become apparent to the reader that their implications in terms of political science, are very significant, not to say momentous, for we are getting very close to what the three writers call "the most intractable of all problems." Yet, unless it does prove tractable, mankind will continue to live in the present nightmare of insecurity.

One last point is stressed in this connection. However it may be composed and whatever its exact functions, the agency might become a public danger as great as that which it would have been created to prevent if it were not subject to the scrutiny and criticism of a body representing the public opinion of the world. The natural body for that purpose also would be the General Assembly of the United Nations, to which the proposed agency, like every other agency of the United Nations, would be under the obligation to report its activities at stated intervals and to send officers to submit to questions and cross-examination in the appropriate Assembly Committee in the presence of the public.

Let us now sum up the issue behind the Baruch Report.

The international control of atomic energy calls for the creation of a small body, numbering not more than twelve and preferably fewer, empowered to make decisions by majority vote. Among the matters on which it will be authorized to make such decisions would be to deal with violators of the atomic treaty, employing force, if necessary.

Such powers have never before been conferred on an international executive body except in the case of relatively unimportant technical issues. Yet, if the Atomic Energy Agency is not entrusted with such powers, the whole purpose for which it was created would be frustrated.

This is what the six Powers meant when they spoke of the issue between those who put sovereignty first and those who are prepared to accept "innovations in traditional concepts of international co-operation, national sovereignty, and economic organization, when these are necessary for security." And this is also what is seen very clearly by the keen-eyed men of the Kremlin.

Under these circumstances, it would have been surprising if the Kremlin had been willing to accept the Baruch Report, for this would have meant signing the death warrant of the Soviet system. This is not to say that the effort to put atomic energy under effective international control must be abandoned. Far from it. Mankind will never enjoy peace and security until the problem of the control of atomic energy and other weapons of mass destruction is solved once and for all, as the Baruch Report has shown that, so far as technical considerations are concerned, it can be. All that the Soviet reaction has revealed is that this problem cannot be solved *in and for itself*, since it cannot be disentangled from the larger problem of the subordination of national sovereignty to the interests of the world as a whole. The Baruch Report may be likened to a reconnaissance made against a stoutly held enemy position. The foe still holds out, more obstinately then ever. But the reconnaissance has proved extremely instructive through the light that it has thrown, not only on the immediate problem to which it was directed but on the larger problem, "the creation," as the British writers put it, "of some form of what, for want of a better name, we call a World State."

It is to this larger problem that we must now address ourselves.

THE UNITED NATIONS CHARTER

SECTION XII

THE UNITED NATIONS CHARTER

"A Constitution to contain an accurate detail of all the subdivisions of which its great powers will admit, and of all the means by which they may be carried into execution, would partake of the prolixity of a legal code and could scarcely be embraced by the human mind. It would probably never be understood by the public. Its nature, therefore, requires that only its great outlines should be marked, its important objects designated, and the minor ingredients which compose these objects should be deduced from the nature of these objects themselves."

— *Chief Justice Marshall in McCulloch* v *Maryland,* 1819

CHAPTER 62: *From Treaty to Constitution*

WE have carried the preparations for the United Nations on the American side, past the Connally and Fulbright Resolutions and the Moscow Conference, up to the point when Secretary of State Cordell Hull was in a position to invite representatives of the leading Powers to take part in preparatory discussions, to be held in a Washington residence known as Dumbarton Oaks, and to lay before them the draft of the plans which had been under discussion in the State Department itself, with leading senators of both parties and with the London, Moscow, and Chungking governments.

205

The American Road to World Peace

The Dumbarton Oaks discussions comprised two phases, since at that time, the summer of 1944, the Soviet government, not being at war with Japan, objected to sitting in conference with the Chinese government. The first phase of the conference, in which the United States, Great Britain, and the Soviet Union participated, took place between August 21 and September 28, 1944, and the second phase, in which the Chinese government participated with the United States and Great Britain, from September 29 to October 7. The results reached at Dumbarton Oaks were embodied in a series of proposals which formed the basis on which the full-dress international conference, which met at San Francisco from April 25 to June 26, 1945, worked out the Charter of the United Nations.

But in order to see the work done at Dumbarton Oaks and at San Francisco in proper perspective, we must stand aside from the details of the 1945 picture and look at the Charter in the light in which history may regard it, as a process of constitutional growth extending over a quarter of a century.

Let us then return briefly to the Europe of 1918, at the time when Woodrow Wilson had first promulgated the words "League of Nations." At that moment, as we have seen, European statesmanship, bereft of its normal instrument of guidance, the balance of power, was intellectually bankrupt. Unable to think in terms of a community of peoples, it could only set itself to devise new kinds of treaties. The British Foreign Office formed a committee composed partly of leading officials from its own ranks and partly of international lawyers and historians. The result of their labors, known as the Phillimore Plan, was a draft treaty which bound the signatories not to go to war with "another of the Allied States" without a process of inquiry and delay. The text of the draft treaty was preceded by a note in the following terms:

> There will be a Preamble reciting that the object of this Convention is to create a League of Nations which will, if possible, prevent all wars in the future.

It is clear that the drafters of the treaty were very far from regarding the League of Nations in the same light as Woodrow Wilson. To them it was merely a new form of alliance between the Great Powers and the extent of their faith in its efficacy is revealed by the words "if possible" which they were frank enough to insert in their suggested preamble.

When we cross the Channel to Paris, we find a very similar frame of mind, but expressing itself in a more rigid and logical form of Treaty. The French foreign minister, too, had appointed a committee to consider the problem of *"La Société des Nations."* It was presided over by an ex-prime minister who had been leader of the French Delegation at the Hague Conference of 1907 and was later the leading French representative in the League of Nations Commission at the Paris Peace Conference. The French Plan, drawn up by this committee, may be described as thoroughly Roman. It proposes the substitution of Right (*droit*) for Force in the settlement of international disputes or conflicts. Legal disputes are to go before an international tribunal (such as had already been proposed at The Hague). All other disputes, including the determination as to what is a legal dispute, would come before a political body which, in effect, would be composed predominantly of representatives of the governments of the Great Powers. This body would both decide the dispute and ensure the execution of the decision; in this latter connection the report enumerates "Sanctions," i.e. forms of enforcement, of various kinds, military sanctions being entrusted to a permanent international general staff, authorized to decide what contingents are to be called upon from individual members of the League.

"The substitution of Right for Force" (*La Paix par le Droit*) is an attractive formula, more appealing than anything in the British Plan. But, looked at closely, neither plan carries one beyond the nineteenth-century Europe of the Great Powers. The British plan was perhaps the more honest, because it did not make play with the word "Justice," when the "judges" would only be the European Great Powers in disguise. But there was nothing in either plan which would mesh in with Woodrow Wilson's thinking or with the American outlook—not a breath of democracy or the faintest suspicion of idealism, the idealism which Woodrow Wilson was at that very moment evoking in the breasts of millions of Europeans.

How was it then that what resulted from Woodrow Wilson's labors in Paris, although necessarily cast in treaty form, was much more than a treaty, was, in fact, an *institution?* How was it that London and Paris and Rome joined together with Washington in framing something which had in it a breath of life and out of which, in due time, developed the United Nations Charter?

It was because, as we have already said in dealing with the Fourteen Points, the League of Nations contained what the old nineteenth-century treaties never provided, arrangements for *a permanent organization.*

The credit for this side of the work of 1919 cannot be ascribed solely to Woodrow Wilson, since, "arrangements for regular conference" are provided for in a British Foreign Office paper produced quite independently of the Phillimore Plan and labeled in Hunter Miller's volume of League of Nations documents as "the Cecil Plan." On both sides of the Atlantic forward-looking minds realized that the best way of overcoming, or circumventing, the intellectual bankruptcy of the chancelleries was by creating institutions which would bring together fresh minds, or experienced minds in fresh surroundings, and so start a process of development which might in time bring into being institutions with a momentum of their own, institutions of which the statesmen of a later generation might make use in ways as yet unpredictable.

It would be too much to say that already at that time the British, who had so much to do with the framing and early tending of these institutions, thought of the Covenant of the League of Nations as an embryo world constitution. All that they were conscious of was that they were starting something which might *grow,* as British institutions have "grown." But, looking back from the vantage point of 1952, we can see them in that light today; and it was therefore quite natural that when Secretary of State Stettinius wrote his report to the President on the Results of the San

Francisco Conference, he should divide his introductory analysis into two parts: the Charter "in its capacity as declaration and the Charter in its capacity as constitution." The transition from treaty to constitution had been accomplished—at least in the minds of the representatives of the United States. It is from that standpoint, therefore, that we shall conduct our analysis of the organs of the United Nations.

CHAPTER 63: *The Constitutional Pattern*

A constitution is not a miscellaneous collection of social rules or "laws." It is a definite piece of social construction, embodying a recognized pattern. Any despot can frame social rules and call them laws. But laws, in the true sense of that word, are *constitutional* rules, and this implies that there is a permanent constitution behind them. To the Greeks, the originators of constitutional government, a constitution (*politeia*) was, in its original meaning, an abstract term, denoting the political quality, or what we should today call the way of life, of the community, democratic or aristocratic as the case might be. But when the political thinkers began to analyze what their predecessors, the creators, had accomplished, they discerned in it a pattern. Since this pattern is, let us say so boldly, the *right* pattern, a pattern which corresponds to the nature of the public affairs with which constitutions are brought into existence to deal, it has become an orthodox or standard pattern, one to which all modern constitution-makers, whether they are true constitutionalists or not, feel it right and expedient to conform. Thus the Soviet Union has a constitution framed according to the standard prescriptions and nobody reading it, and unfamiliar with the conditions in that country, could guess that those who hold power there are totally unable to understand the meaning of the words: "the Rule of Law."

According to this pattern, the constitutional "way of life" requires provision for a legislature, an executive, and a judiciary. As a recent writer puts it: "In a unitary government . . . the constitution needs to provide no more than the structure, in general terms, of the legislature, the executive, and the judiciary; the nature, in broad outline, of their mutual relations; and the nature of their relations to the community itself."

Let us apply this clear and concise formulation to the United Nations Charter, dealing with its institutions in the order given above: first the legislature, then the executive, then the judiciary, and finally their mutual relations and their relations to the peoples behind them, that is, to the United Nations themselves.

CHAPTER 64: *The Legislature:*
Its Place in the Constitution

THE legislature, in a modern state, is the governmental organ which is in the closest and most direct touch with the people. In ancient Greece it comprised the entire free male adult population, and the practice of "direct democracy," as it is called, is still to be found in some Swiss cantons and in the time-honored New England town meeting. But, apart from such occasional survivals, the modern legislature is not a meeting *of the people*, in the strict sense, but a meeting emanating *from the people*, through the use of the representative process.

The powers of such a representative body depend upon the exact pattern of the constitution; for on this point there is no standard type. In some states, of which Great Britain is a good example, the representative body, or Parliament, controls the executive. The ministers, or members of what is called "the Government—that is to say, the executive branch—occupy front-bench seats in Parliament, as the foremost representatives of their political party, and the life of the government depends upon its retaining the confidence of the elected assembly. At any moment, Parliament, by a vote of "no confidence," can bring that relationship to an end.

In other states, where the principle of "the Separation of Powers" has been adopted in the Constitution, as in the United States, the legislature, or Congress, has no direct control over the executive, but carries on its functions independently, in the absence of the executive members. This does not mean that the executive and the legislature are entirely separated from one another: in the close interdependence of all public affairs this could not possibly be. It only means that the relationship between these two branches of the government is not organic, in the sense that the control of the executive by the legislature is laid down in the Constitution, but that it is left to be regulated according to the circumstances at any given time or by understandings or other arrangements outside the letter of the Constitution.

CHAPTER 65: *The Legislature:*
Its Evolution and Membership

THE United Nations Charter, as we shall see, makes ample provision for the legislative process on the international level. Yet it is not easy to discern in the Covenant of the League of Nations the germ out of which all this activity was to spring.

The Phillimore Plan ignored the legislative process altogether: treaties of guarantee belong to a wholly different realm from that of elected parliaments. The Cecil Plan opens the door a little way in a very cautious manner, characteristic of the relations between the chancelleries and popular assemblies in nineteenth-century Europe. "There might," it said, "be a periodical congress of delegates of parliaments of the states belonging to the League, as a development out of the existing Interparliamentary Union. A regular staple of discussion for this body would be afforded by the reports of the Inter-State Conference and of the different international bodies. The Congress would thus cover the ground which is at present occupied by the periodical Hague Conference and also, perhaps, the ground claimed by the Socialist International." It is to be noted that the word "congress," as employed above, is not used in the familiar American parliamentary sense, but is applied to the full-dress meetings of large-scale international organizations, official or nonofficial; the latter, it should be remembered, were then much less numerous, and much less influential in public opinion, than they have since become. Had this not been so, the idea that the ground which they occupy could be "covered" by an organ of the League of Nations could never have been seriously put forward.

The article in the Covenant containing what we may call the embryo of the United Nations Legislature consists of four brief paragraphs:

1. The Assembly shall consist of Representatives of the Members of the League.

2. The Assembly shall meet at stated intervals and from time to time as occasion may require at the Seat of the League or at such other place as may be decided upon.

3. The Assembly may deal at its meetings with any matter within the sphere of action of the League or affecting the peace of the world.

4. At meetings of the Assembly, each member of the League shall have one vote, and may not have more than three representatives.

Looked at in the perspective of a third of a century, what seems most noteworthy in this Article are its omissions. It does not provide for annual meetings, since the "stated intervals" may be intervals of any length, and it does not specify what matters the Assembly is to deal with. For instance, it ignores the problem of finance:

212

and control over finance, as every student of constitutional history knows, is one of the chief means through which parliaments have extended their powers. Nor does it say anything about the relationship between the Assembly and any other organ of the League—for example, the Council.

According to Article 5 of the Covenant, the first meeting of the Assembly was to be "summoned by the President of the United States of America." When Woodrow Wilson had carried out this statutory duty, in circumstances very different from those anticipated by the framers of the Covenant, and the Assembly came together in September, 1920, it lost no time in putting life into those four dry paragraphs.

It was discovered that, even without the invigorating influence of the United States, there was an abundant store of political energy which had never been tapped by the nineteenth-century system and was now available for use at Geneva. These newcomers to the official international scene consisted chiefly of representatives of the smaller states, which had been pushed into the background under the old power-political diplomatic arrangements. Among these were European states, some of which, like Belgium and Greece, had played an honored part in the war, while others, such as Holland, Spain, Switzerland, Norway, Denmark, and Sweden had remained neutral; then there were the states of Latin America, eleven of which had been belligerents and had therefore become original members of the League, while six others had been at once invited to "accede to the Covenant"; a few others, notably Mexico, came in somewhat later. Then there were isolated states, such as Iran (still known as "Persia"), China, Siam, Hedjaz in Asia, and Liberia in Africa, forerunners of others in their regions in the future; and finally, last but not least, the self-governing "Dominions" of what was then still called "the British Empire," together with India which, although not self-governing, secured admittance as an "original member" without her qualifications being submitted to examination.

The result was that there was brought together in 1920 a collection of some thirty states which, viewed as a whole, was very different from the relatively homogeneous "family of states" which the older writers on international law had in mind when they laid out the rules of their social behavior.

The first full-dress modern gathering of "sovereign" states was that which drew up the Treaty of Westphalia in 1648—a treaty named after a province rather than after a town, because susceptibilities about rank and precedence prevented some of the leading members from residing under conditions where they would be exposed to embarrassing contacts. All the Westphalian signatories were European and, at least nominally, Christian. So too were the signatories of the Vienna Treaty of 1815. It was not until the settlement following the Crimean War of 1854 that Turkey, then a Moslem State, was admitted into the privileged circle. Japan followed at the end of the nineteenth century. When the first Hague Conference met in 1899 there were doubts in the minds of some traditionally inclined diplomats whether the Latin-American states should be invited; but the broader view prevailed. Such narrow notions were, of course, entirely foreign to the mind of Woodrow Wilson and there is no trace of them in the League of Nations Covenant. Nevertheless, a certain exclusiveness still persisted among the representatives of the European Great Powers and made itself felt in the meetings and other contacts of the Council of the League of Nations. It was resentment against this attitude of mind, more than any particular political grievance, which led to the retirement of Brazil from the League of Nations in 1926.

Thus, in spite of the many recent additions to the "Family of Nations," the League of Nations was predominantly European in character and "white" in pigmentation. The non-Europeans and the "nonwhites" were still, in the eyes of those accustomed to the older diplomatic tradition, "outsiders." Woodrow Wilson had an opportunity of striking a blow at this had he been willing to accept the Japanese proposal for a form of words in the Preamble of the Covenant embodying the principle of racial equality, but he let the occasion slip by.

In the United Nations the problem of membership presents itself in a wholly new light. As the record stands in 1952, of its sixty members only ten are European, while sixteen are Asian and twenty Latin American. Its African membership, which now stands at four, is likely to be much enlarged in the coming years, as various ex-colonial territories acquire qualifications for membership. The Gold Coast and Nigeria, in particular, are already approaching that stage. This enumeration takes no account of the Soviet Union and such of its component or conquered territories as have been admitted to membership; but, however they may be classed, it cannot be claimed that they reinforce the older diplomatic tradition.

Thus the European States have become rather a small minority in the total membership of the United Nations. Diminished in power, they are also diminished in what used to constitute social prestige. All the greater is the responsibility laid upon them for acquiring influence in new ways and finding fresh opportunities for service in the equal fellowship of member nations.

CHAPTER 66: *The Legislature:*
The Economic and Social Council
and the Specialized Agencies

WE have said that the United Nations makes ample provision for the legislative process. But it does not do this directly. Indeed, in his San Francisco Report, Secretary of State Stettinius affirms the contrary. "It will be the responsibility of the general assembly," he says, "to discuss, debate, reveal, expose, lay open—to perform, that is, the healthful and ventilating functions of a free deliberative body without the right or duty to enact or to legislate." Certainly in the assembly sessions that have already been held these "healthful and ventilating functions" have been abundantly exercised and will continue to be so more and more, as technological advance enables the citizens of the member nations to participate in the proceedings by eye and ear, irrespective of distance. From this point of view, the phrase applied to the General Assembly, "the town meeting of the world" is acquiring a meaning undreamed of by the older political thinkers. Through the General Assembly, with its complete freedom for the expression and interchange of diverse views, the member countries can be educated in a sense of responsibility, a consensus of opinion worthy to be described as "the public opinion of mankind" can be brought into being and furnished with lasting standards and values, and, above all, means can be found, whenever the occasion arises, for mobilizing the conscience of the whole world on behalf of these values.

But this is only one side of the General Assembly. Let us return to it in its capacity as a legislative body.

This is set forth in Chapter IX of the Charter under the heading of "International Economic and Social Co-operation." All legislation in a free country is, of course, a process of co-operation; thus there is no difference of *kind* between legislation on the national and on the international level. It is only the methods which differ—and these differ considerably on the national level also.

By Article 60 the Charter vests authority for this work of international economic and social co-operation in the General Assembly. But, as has already been said, this body does not carry out this work directly—such a task would be far too complex and one quite unsuited to it—but through a special organ, the Economic and Social Council. Nor does this last-named body itself deal directly with any but major problems of international life. Generally speaking, international legislation is carried out through the so-called Specialized Agencies, now twelve in number. How large a volume of such legislation already exists on what may be called the world's statute book most citizens of individual countries are little aware. We have already touched on this realm in speaking of the World Services. These have been greatly developed and extended under the United Nations system and it is literally true to say that there is no single person who is today qualified to express an informed judgment on how their work as a whole is being carried on; for each Agency is an autonomous body working under a constitution of its own and dealing with tasks which it requires particular knowledge and experience to evaluate. Each has a climate and atmosphere, and is developing a set of habits, which will result in time in a tradition of its own. In some cases, such as the realm of labor, covered by the International Labor Organization, these interests affect a large section of the community and can be brought to the notice of citizens in the member countries through national and local bodies, such as labor unions and associations of industrialists. Somewhat the same may be said of UNESCO, the United Nations Educational, Scientific, and Cultural Organization, which was created to deal with the things of the mind in their various aspects. A typical example of the legislative process in this connection has lately been afforded by the Universal Copyright Convention signed in Geneva on September 6, 1952, as a result of a conferences convened by UNESCO.

Like all such international agreements, this has, of course, still to be ratified according to the constitutional processes of the individual states concerned. But this does not detract from the legislative quality of the work. On the contrary, it is a valuable safeguard, like the existence of two chambers in the national legislative domain. Nothing could be less democratic than to circumvent national parliaments by slipping in new laws with new social responsibilities by the back door.

In the case of the more technical topics for which Specialized Agencies have been set up, such as Health, Food and Agriculture, Telecommunications, Civil Aviation, and Metereology, it is difficult for the plain citizen to follow the detailed proceedings and he has to rely on the conscience and public spirit of the experts to maintain their own standards. How to bring the democratic process effectively into play in these specialized realms is a problem which is still largely unsolved. Indeed it cannot be fully solved until the United Nations has succeeded in its major task, the organization of peace, and its subsidiary organs and activities are thus set free to work unhindered by extraneous influences in their own allotted fields.

IN performing the functions which have just been described, functions of legislation and deliberation, the General Assembly, like its predecessor, the Assembly of the League of Nations, has been hampered by the existence of another body for which place was found in the constitution. This awkward neighbor was known in the League Covenant by the comprehensive title of "The Council," while in the United Nations system it bears the more restricted name of "The Security Council."

This restriction marks an important milestone in the constitutional evolution of the World Authority. Under the system of the Covenant, into which, as we have seen, the Assembly was introduced by an afterthought as a kind of appendage, the legislative process embodied in the World Services was placed under the supervision of this "Council." The Assembly was indeed free to discuss the work of what were then known as "the Technical Organizations," but the control and responsibility rested with the Council, to which their annual reports were submitted for approval. As, after 1925, the Council was mainly occupied with matters of high policy, its members were little interested in the so-called "technical" subjects and were also, as a rule, not at all well qualified to deal with them. Indeed, in some cases, particular states used these technical agencies for their own nationalistic purposes, thus interfering with their inner working; for at that time the autonomy guaranteed to the Specialized Agencies under the United Nations system had not yet been established and, by the system which divided up the business of the Council among *rapporteurs*, it was possible for individual countries to acquire something of a private domain of their own and thus to build up what amounted to a vested interest.

These unsatisfactory conditions formed the subject of a League Inquiry in the late thirties and its conclusions, embodied in the

Bruce Report (so called from the name of its Australian chairman), doubtless exercised some influence on the framers of the Charter. However this may be, the Charter made a clear cut between the body which took the place of the League Council and the domain of social and economic affairs. The outward and visible symbol of this is the Economic and Social Council, on which all members of the United Nations stand on an equal footing, as they do in the General Assembly.

But, to return to the question of the awkward neighbor, under the Covenant system there was no relationship whatsoever laid down between the Assembly and the Council. This was deliberately kept vague and left to be decided pragmatically by the force of events.

Such an arrangement, which would have seemed strange to the Fathers of the United States Constitution, had the merit of enabling the statesmen who used the Geneva machine to feel their way by trying various constitutional experiments. This was particularly so in the early years, when the foreign ministers had not yet acquired the habit of visiting Geneva, but were conducting their power-political business either from their foreign office desks or through the Conference of Ambassadors, which was the prolongation of the Paris Peace Conference.

During those years, when Eastern Europe and Western Asia were a sea of troubles, Geneva was an island of calm. The Secretariat, cut off from the more responsible tasks in the organization of peace, was using this period of relative inactivity in order to develop the technical activities or World Services of which Geneva had become the co-ordinating center; and the smaller Powers, for their part, were making the most of their new international responsibilities, to which the Europeans among them, at any rate, were determined to address themselves very seriously.

A special word of tribute is due in this connection to the first President of the Assembly, Paul Hymans, then Foreign Minister of Belgium, a tried constitutionalist who acquitted himself so well in his Geneva post that he had the unusual honor of being elected to it again in 1932. It was Hymans, who, after having taken contact with the delegates and the public, young and old, who accompanied them, remarked, with characteristic penetration, that there seemed to be as many different concepts of the League of Nations as there were countries in its membership.

But Europe, and indeed the whole world, had to pay a heavy price for having failed, under the nineteenth-century system, to draw upon the services of the smaller states and thus to accustom them to bearing their proportionate burden of responsibility for world affairs. For they now found it very difficult to divest themselves of their habitual attitude as bystanders and critics; and in this they found support unfortunately not only among their own peoples but also among certain sections of public opinion in some of the Great Power countries. It was a combination of such irresponsible elements which launched the Assembly on the long and futile quest for "disarmament" to which reference has already been made. The illusions on which this policy was based were only finally blown away by the German invasion of Norway and Denmark in 1940.

It is instructive to look back on this period from the angle of political science. The World Services are, each of them, miniature international organizations, but organizations in which the element of power is reduced to a minimum. The more technical they are, the less, generally speaking, the element of power tends to enter in. These services have developed according to the model fixed at the Postal Conference of 1874, which originated what has been known since 1878 as the Universal Postal Union. There is a conference meeting once every few years, which is, within the range of the organization, supreme, or, if one chooses to use the word, sovereign. There is an executive, which meets at more frequent intervals and keeps the organization going between conferences; and there is a permanent staff or secretariat at headquarters.

There were times at Geneva in the early twenties when the Assembly was beginning to regard itself as the sovereign conference of a number of world services and the League Council as an executive under its control. There were discussions in the Assembly, for instance, on matters dealt with in the Council, such as the treatment of minorities, and there was at least one occasion when the Chairman of the Council for the time being, who happened to be a member of one of the smaller European states, went to the tribune to defend and explain the Council's action, using the first person plural in referring to the policy adopted by his colleagues and himself. He was, in fact, speaking as a Cabinet Minister, under the system of responsible government, would address the Parliament which had a right to call him to account and, if things came to the test, to dismiss him.

This process of constitutional experimentation was rudely interrupted in 1925, when the foreign ministers of Britain, France, and Germany began to make it their habit to visit Geneva. The World Services went on, but they were pushed into the background, and with it the close collaboration between the team of high officials in the Secretariat which was beginning to give Geneva a name all the world over for true international co-operation. The divisive forces of power-politics entered in. The foreign ministers brought their own experts with them, in particular their legal experts, and as one of the original secretariat team in the Political Section remarked sadly at the time: "Now there is nothing for us to do but to arrange the pencils and the blotting pads."

But this was not the last effort of the small states to assert the authority of the Assembly against their overmighty superiors in the Council. In 1924, because of the presence of the British and French foreign ministers, the Assembly had embarked on a very ambitious effort. It had tried to solve the triple problem—as it was then conceived—of arbitration, security, and disarmament in a single document, known as the Geneva Protocol, a sort of improved Covenant with the loopholes carefully stopped up. It is still an open question whether, if this document had been more skillfully handled—withdrawn, for instance, for further consideration in the following session—it might not have bridged the gulf between Britain and France. However that may be, the Protocol was rejected by a different British government in 1925 and the British, French, and German foreign ministers retired to a Swiss health resort, Locarno, to frame an alternative plan on more limited lines.

The American Road to World Peace

This retreat from Geneva annoyed some of the smaller Powers and they gave vent to this feeling in the Assembly of 1925. Here was a new alignment—the small Powers ranged against the Great. But the revolt did not last long; for, on second thoughts, the small states realized that the Great Powers held them in the hollow of their hands, if they chose to assert their power.

After having been thus rudely called to order, the smaller states settled down perforce to playing the role of spectators or satellites in that long-drawn-out debating match between Britain and France which led, after the depression of 1929, through Manchuria, Ethiopia, the Rhineland, and Munich, to the dissolution of the League. In these proceedings, during which the smaller states had their powerlessness painfully borne in upon them, the Assembly played the part of a helpless bystander.

What, the reader may ask, has all this to do with the General Assembly of the United Nations?

The answer is that it has a great deal to do with it: for it is an object lesson revealing the choice which lies before the United States today as a Great Power in the United Nations system. Will the United States stand on its prerogatives as a Great Power, once again recognized in the Charter, as in the League of Nations Covenant, or will it do, what the League Great Powers never did, and never could do, because of their power-political traditions, assume the leadership of all the states, the smaller as well as the greater, making use of the General Assembly for its exercise?

Because of the nonco-operative attitude of the Soviet Union in thwarting the Security Council, American statesmanship has found it easy to answer this question. It has not only thrown in its lot with all the member states, both great and small, but it has been instrumental in enlarging the functions of the General Assembly so that it now exercises responsibilities which, though they were theoretically open to the League Assembly under the Covenant, were in practice quite beyond its power to assume. The absence of the representative of the Soviet Union from the Security Council on June 25 and 27, 1950, enabled the United Nations to set on foot measures to repel aggression on Korea. When, "because of lack of unanimity of the permanent members," the Security Council "failed to exercise its primary responsibility for the maintenance of international peace and security," and the General Assembly took this responsibility on to its own shoulders, a momentous step was taken in the constitutional development of the United Nations. It was faced for the first time with the question whether the Security Council was really a necessary part of the United Nations system, or whether, in fact, it was not perhaps an encumbrance which might be stripped off with advantage to the organization as a whole.

But before we form a judgment on this question, we must look more closely at the Security Council and its predecessor, the Council of the League of Nations.

CHAPTER 68: *A Misshapen Organ*

TO reach an answer to the question raised at the end of the last chapter, we must once more cast our minds back to 1919.

The concept of the League of Nations as an institution rather than as a mere treaty originated, as we have seen, both with Woodrow Wilson and with the British Foreign Office. But the formulation of this concept was due to British draftsmanship. The Foreign Office draftsman conceived of the League as being no more, and no less, than a nineteenth-century diplomatic conference equipped with permanent machinery, in the form of a secretariat and fixed arrangements for regular meetings, and established in a neutral center, Geneva. The word "Council," which suggests a corporate personality, is studiously avoided. The Cecil Plan speaks throughout of an "Interstate Conference."

This plan was circulated to the members of the British War Cabinet and approved by it on December 17, 1918, as an outline of the British plan for the proposed League of Nations, to be used in the impending Paris Peace Conference.

But in the interval between its circulation to the members of the War Cabinet and its dispatch to Paris, an incident occurred which has had a lasting effect upon the development of international political organization. General Smuts, the South African statesman, was at that time a member of the War Cabinet and thus read the Foreign Office paper before the meeting on December 17. Not only did he read it, but he assimilated it so thoroughly that on December 16 he signed the foreword of an essay which was published shortly afterwards under the title *The League of Nations: A Practical Suggestion*. This essay, he explained, had been "hastily written at the last moment . . . in view of the early meeting of the Peace Conference."

In its main lines, and particularly in viewing the League of Nations as an institution rather than as a treaty, the Smuts essay reinforced the argument of the Cecil Plan. Indeed, in some cases the actual wording was followed. But on certain points he diverged from it and unfortunately these were important enough to ruin the working of the plan in the form in which it had been conceived.

The Smuts essay is reprinted in Hunter Miller's documentary volume and its rather fanciful views on mandates, armaments, and the future of Eastern Europe do not concern us here. The point on which his intervention proved of lasting and harmful effect was in his treatment of the "Interstate Conference" of the Cecil Plan.

He made this his own, renamed it the Council of the League and increased its membership by four additional representatives, who, of course, would not be Great Powers. The Council would thus, as he saw it, consist of two classes of members: the Great Powers would be "permanent members," while the other four would be temporary.

Now, anyone familiar with the psychology of international diplomacy at that time would have been aware that the statesmen of the Great Powers would never demean themselves to meeting on equal terms, and transacting important business, with the representatives of smaller states. This was a thing which had "never been done" in European diplomacy. It was not done in Vienna in 1815, the precedents of which were being eagerly looked up

in the chancelleries in 1918, and, of course, there was no question
of its now being done in Paris. On the other hand, once the suggestion for the admission of the smaller powers into the proposed
League Council had been made, it was not possible to reject it
outright in the League Commission at the Peace Conference, for
the smaller powers had succeeded in securing representation upon
it. Thus, in spite of some opposition, the plan for a Council composed of permanent and temporary members was adopted and has
been followed in the United Nations Charter. The result was that
the Council never functioned, as Smuts intended that it should, as
"the Executive Committee" of the League. Insofar as there was
an executive functioning in the realm of high international politics during the lifetime of the League, it functioned *outside the
League*, at conferences and in high level diplomatic exchanges
between the Great Powers. The co-operative mechanism, which
the Smuts intervention had unwittingly withdrawn from the
League Council, re-emerged at Locarno, Washington, Stresa,
Rome, and Munich—and even at Geneva, but in the private rooms
of hotels and not under the auspices of the League of Nations.

Thus the so-called Council of the League was doomed from
the first to failure in the role which Smuts had assigned to it. But
there was another and even more serious defect in its misshapen
make-up. Smuts introduced the concept of *elected* members of
the international executive, but he never thought out what that
implied. His suggestions on this point were very lightly sketched.
He contemplated that the four additional members should be
drawn in rotation from two panels, one comprising "the important
intermediate Powers below the rank of Great Powers," among
which he mentions "Spain, Turkey, Central Russia, Poland, and
Greater Serbia," and the other representing "the minor states who
are members of the League." The selection of Council members
from among these was, he said, to be made "according to rules
laid down in the first instance by the permanent members" who,
he added, "will also fix the two original panels."

Little did Smuts realize what an apple of discord he was thus
flinging into the ranks of the society of states—"Great," "Intermediate," and "Minor"—and what temptations to jealousy and

petty rivalry, what opportunities for intrigue and backbiting, he was thus inevitably fostering! Both at Geneva and in the United Nations the prospect of the impending elections has cast its shadow over the scene for months before the Assembly meetings and the statesmen concerned, mindful of their instructions from home, have had to subordinate their duty under the Charter to the requirements of national interest and prestige. In these circumstances, it is asking too much of human nature to expect that the representatives of a candidate state will not make "deals" of some kind, either with the states whose vote he is seeking or with individual Great Powers, if not in both these fields.

Moreover, the influence of this atmosphere of "deals" tends to extend beyond the actual matter at issue, the elected posts on the Council. A very disquieting instance of this, affecting the very basis of the United Nations, occurred recently, when the filling of an elected seat on the Security Council became mixed up with the election of the judges of the International Court of Justice. It had become known that certain Great Powers favored the election to the Court, in place of a Latin-American judge who had died, of a national of a country, India, which had not previously been represented there. The Latin-American caucus, unwilling to sacrifice what it considered to be part of its legitimate patronage, reacted by blocking the election of the candidate favored by the United States to one of the two elected seats on the Security Council. A deadlock ensued which it took over thirty ballots to overcome, and, in the effort to do so with satisfaction to both parties in the tussle, one of the most distinguished judges in the Court, who happened to be standing for reelection, became an innocent victim.

The argument is sometimes heard that this element in the procedure of the United Nations is "democratic." This is a false use of that term. There is nothing democratic about the election of one state by a group of states to fill a vacancy on an international body. A state thus elected is in no sense a representative. Its government would be betraying its signature under the Charter, as well as its duty to its own people, if it conceived itself to be so. Every member of the Security Council or of any other United

Nations organ is in duty bound to carry on its activities in the interest of the United Nations Organization as a whole and of its principles and purposes, as laid down in the Charter. It is one of the many harmful results that have followed from the adoption of the ill-considered Smuts proposal that it has weakened the sense of United Nations loyalty among the members of the Security Council and thus thwarted the constitutional progress of that body, which would have been difficult enough to ensure in any case.

CHAPTER 69: *The Record of the Security Council*

WE can now return to the question which was left unanswered at the close of Chapter 67: Is the Security Council really a necessary part of the United Nations Organization, or has it not, on the contrary, become an encumbrance, which could be removed with advantage to the institution as a whole?

Let us begin by asking what is the place which, constitutionally speaking, the Security Council was designed to occupy, both in the League Covenant and in the United Nations Charter. The answer is clear. In the three-fold division of constitutional functions on the world level, the Assembly represents the Legislature, the International Court of Justice the Judiciary, and the Security Council the *Executive*. This is made explicit in Article 24 of the Charter, under which, "in order to ensure prompt and effective action by the United Nations, its members confer on the Security Council primary responsibility for the maintenance of international peace and security and agree that in carrying out its duties under this responsibility the Security Council acts on their behalf."

By subscribing to these last words, United Nations members not represented on the Council (and as we have just said, no one state on the Council is capable of representing any other state) made a great concession, or, as it would be more appropriate to say, a great step forward in world integration. They abandoned their independence (let us drop the word "sovereignty") so far as the issue of war and peace, or what is now called "the maintenance of international peace and security," is concerned. This is an advance the significance of which has perhaps not been sufficiently appreciated by students of world affairs, though, in actual fact, it is, of course only a wise and necessary adjustment to international conditions as they now are. It is an advance that parallels the advance made by the government of the United States, when it announced its willingness to submit itself to the conditions of the Baruch Report, which included readiness to accept the decision of a vetoless enforcement agency.

We can therefore begin our discussion of the executive function in the Charter by laying it down that all the members of the United Nations except the Soviet Union—the one Great Power which has refused to accept the Baruch Report—recognize the need for an organ which will carry out the purpose that executive bodies carry out at every level from a parish council or a local sports club upwards, namely to "ensure prompt and effective action" on behalf of the members of the larger body for which it acts. In the case of the Executive of the United Nations, its particular, though by no means its sole, purpose is to "maintain and, if necessary, restore international peace and security."

Has the Security Council carried out this purpose? Has it shown itself to be a true executive body?

The answer, of course, is that it has proved itself to be so unable to carry out its declared purpose under the Charter that its functions have been increasingly handed over to other bodies. This supersession of its activities has taken place in two ways, firstly through the increasing use of the General Assembly in security matters and, secondly, through the development of regional systems of defense.

These two large modifications in the working of the Charter have been brought about in large measure through the persistently nonco-operative attitude of the Soviet Union and, in particular, through its use of the veto power on which it insisted at the

Dumbarton Oaks and San Francisco Conferences as the indispensable price for its adherence to the United Nations. It is hardly necessary to recall that the Soviet Union has used its veto in the Security Council on more than fifty occasions.

The tendency to refer to the General Assembly matters on which the Security Council had been unable to reach a positive decision began early in the life of the United Nations. The Spanish question was so referred in 1946 and the Greek question in 1947. Later on, the question of the disposition of the Italian colonies came before the Assembly because the Great Powers had failed to reach agreement on it when the Italian Peace Treaty was being negotiated. In much the same way, the question of the observance of human rights in Bulgaria, Hungary, and Rumania passed to the Assembly after the failure of efforts to implement the provisions of the peace treaties with these countries in regard to those rights. Only one further example need be mentioned: the uncertain handling of the Palestine question in the Security Council in the spring of 1948.

These instances, particularly the last-named, illustrate the fact that the difficulties in the Security Council were not due entirely to Soviet obstruction. They stemmed also from disagreements, sometimes deep-seated disagreements, between the Western Powers, but they were exacerbated and rendered more difficult of solution by the presence of the Soviet Union, which was always ready to inject its dose of acid into any controversy. The record of the Security Council affords convincing proof—if proof was needed—that the old nineteenth-century method of the "Supremacy of the Great Powers" has outlived its usefulness and that it cannot be satisfactorily adjusted to the conditions of the age which opened in 1945. Strange as it would have seemed to Palmerston, Metternich, and Bismarck, an assembly of representatives of sixty states, most of them individually of minor importance, has succeeded in carrying out practical achievements like the federation of Ethiopia and Eritrea and the creation of the state of Libya where the Great Powers had failed.

When we survey the record of the Security Council as a whole, leaving aside the Soviet Union and bearing in mind the difficulties with which the Western Powers have had to contend, we cannot honestly regard it as commendable. Two causes, in particular, contribute to this unfavorable conclusion. One is that the Council has been reluctant to take its stand positively and definitely on the Rule of Law; and the second, which is closely related to the first, is that the Council has neglected to provide itself with satisfactory rules of procedure.

The question of the relation of the Security Council to the Rule of Law goes back to the San Francisco Conference, where a number of delegates—among whom Mr. Evatt, the Australian Minister of External Affairs, was the most prominent—took strong exception to the fact the Dumbarton Oaks draft of the Charter gave no guidance of principle to the Security Council on which to base its decisions for peaceful settlement. As the smaller states have discovered to their cost, "peaceful settlements" imposed by the Great Powers may be contrary to the most elementary principles of justice. The Munich Agreement of 1938 is a flagrant recent example of a tendency which goes back to the partitions of Poland and beyond.

As laid down in the Dumbarton Oaks draft, the first purpose of the United Nations was to be:

> To maintain international peace and security; and to that end to take effective collective measures for the prevention and removal of threats to the peace and the suppression of acts of aggression or other breaches of the peace, and *to bring about by peaceful means adjustment or settlement* of international disputes which may lead to a breach of the peace.

As Mr. Evatt records in his book on the United Nations, published in 1948, Australians "with the enthusiastic cooperation and support of the other middle and smaller nations, but only after a most strenuous and, at times, bitter fight," succeeded in modifying these words and in changing the Dumbarton Oaks draft in certain other respects. The San Francisco version of the first purpose of the United Nations reads as follows:

The United Nations Charter

To maintain collective peace and security, and to that end to take effective collective measures for the prevention and removal of threats to the peace, and for the suppression of acts of aggression and other breaches of the peace, and to bring about by peaceful means, *and in conformity with the principles of justice and international law*, adjustment or settlement of international disputes or situations which might lead to a breach of the peace.

The words inserted at San Francisco, italicized in the above extract, seemed sufficient to prevent the Security Council from acting in an arbitrary manner.

At the time when he wrote his book Mr. Evatt was evidently under that impression. But other authorities, who have watched the working of the Security Council at close range, do not share this hopeful view. In the 1951 issue of the *Annual Review of United Nations Affairs*, issued by the New York University Graduate Program of Studies in cooperation with the Department of Public Information of the United Nations, its editor, Professor Clyde Eagleton, complains that, in spite of the San Francisco amendment,

> ... the Security Council was given no rules of law to guide it in deciding who is the aggressor; it can call anybody an aggressor if it has votes enough to do it. There is no law in the procedure at all. The emphasis was on the political side at the beginning and the United Nations has developed in that direction since then. The organs of the United Nations have not called on the International Court for decisions or advisory opinions interpreting the Charter, and in practice the rule now is that each interprets the Charter for itself: there is no judicial review.

Even more impressive, since it comes from one who has actually participated in the work of the Security Council, is the testimony of Mr. Paul Hasluck, former Counsellor-in-charge of the Australian Mission to the United Nations and Acting Representative on the Security Council, in his volume entitled the *Workshop of Security* published in 1947. He writes:

There would appear to be a danger in the possibility that the Council can exercise very wide powers without restraint. If the Great Powers were acting in concert, they would undoubtedly find a most potent instrument ready to hand. All that they would need to complete their constitutional domination of the world would be the support of five nonpermanent members. Then they could, in effect, "give orders" to other nations and invoke the the Charter to see that they were carried out.

Mr. Hasluck's phrase, "the constitutional domination of the world," illustrates how far educated public opinion has moved since 1914. Up to that time, the "domination of the world" by the Great Powers was the generally accepted recipe for the maintenance of peace, and in 1918 Europeans who considered themselves forward-looking wished to make this domination "constitutional" by providing a framework for it by means of the League of Nations. But today the peoples are very much more alive and are no longer prepared to take "orders" from the Great Powers unless they are based on "principles of justice and international law." It is safe to predict that these words will before long become as familiar to Americans as the words "due process of law" in the Fifth Amendment.

We come now to the question of the Security Council's procedure. This may seem at first sight to be a minor matter; but as all students of constitutional government know, it is really of prime importance, for principles have a way of developing out of customary procedures, and even out of provisional arrangements adopted through gaps in procedures formally laid down. No shrewder way of thwarting the healthy development of an institution could be devised than to cripple its working by subjecting it to faulty procedures. The agents of the Soviet Union are adepts in the arts of procedure, of which the older generation among them learned to make full use during their conspiratorial days. They have not failed to use this experience in their seat on the Security Council.

Most people will remember the month of August, 1950, when for four long weeks Jacob Malik occupied the Chair in the Security Council and through his mastery in the arts of stultification prevented that body from doing a single stroke of business. Many may have wondered how it was possible for him to do so. It was not only because of his skill in maneuver at the time. It was also because the existing rules of the Council made it possible for a President to do so without any effective interference from his colleagues or from some higher authority. In effect, he was for a month dictator of the most powerful organ in the United Nations, prepared like Nero, to let the world burn while he exercised his skill on a favorite instrument.

There has been a more recent incident of the same kind which, though less scandalous, must have caused misgivings in many quarters. This was the debate in the Security Council in April, 1952, on the question whether the problem of Tunis should be inscribed on its agenda. This was a matter which occasioned deep perplexity both to the United States and to the British representatives and, in the event, they cast their votes in different ways: the British vote was cast in the negative and the United States abstained. When the motion failed for lack of the necessary seven affirmative votes, its sponsors made no secret of the fact that they felt aggrieved. And well they might be, for the objections which were voiced by the representatives of certain countries against the discussion of "matters of domestic jurisdiction" in the Security Council, and indeed in the United Nations generally, had been overruled on previous occasions. The advocates of Tunisian rights could not be expected to forget that a proposal to put the Indonesian question on the agenda of the Council was made in 1946— and not even by a regular member of the Council but by the Ukrainian government, which claimed to have a special interest in the matter under Article 31 of the Charter, and that its claim was allowed and the discussion granted.

Article 2 paragraph 7 lays it down that "nothing in the present Charter shall authorize the United Nations to intervene in matters which are essentially within the domestic jurisdiction of any state or shall require the members to submit such matters to settlement under the present Charter." What do these words mean? Can a line be drawn, other than the danger of a threat to the peace, between matters on which "intervention" by the United Nations is or is not admissible; and where "intervention" would not be admissible, would *discussion* in the General Assembly or other organs of the UN be in order?

This is a matter which cannot be left much longer in the twilight in which it is at present enveloped, especially now that the countries of Latin America, Asia, and the Middle East, who tend to hold strong views on it, have acquired the habit of acting together in the General Assembly, where they constitute a majority of its membership. A ruling from the Court, giving some guidance on the interpretation of the clause, would seem to be overdue in order to prevent future procedural contradictions.

In conclusion, a word must be said about the way in which the President of the Council is chosen. Under Article 30 of the Charter the Council was left free to "adopt its own rules of procedure, including the method of selecting its President." The present method is that of monthly rotation according to the alphabetical order of the states members. This was taken over, without further question, from the Executive Committee of the Preparatory Commission of 1945 and, as was only to be expected, it has led to great inequality in the performance of the duties of this office. This would not have been so serious a matter if the President had had adequate guidance laid down for him in the rules of procedure or if he had had at his elbow an experienced and trustworthy officer of the UN Secretariat. On this latter point let us once more cite Professor Eagleton, who, in his latest annual review, in referring to this question, remarks that "a particular problem in this respect is that the Assistant Secretary General for Security Affairs is a Russian and will probably continue to be one." And then, with a side glance at the war in Korea, he continues: "How can the strategy of the United Nations against an ally of Russia be conducted if this strategy and intelligence flow through a department of the United Nations commanded by a Russian? A political command of some kind will have to wrestle with that problem."

WE saw in the last chapter that the chief function of the executive branch of the United Nations, that of dealing with aggression or the threat of aggression, had fallen into other hands. Constitutions, like Nature, abhor a vacuum, and when the Security Council ceased to perform its allotted task, the General Assembly and the regional authorities brought into existence under Article 51 took over. But this was not a solution of the problem involved in the breakdown of the executive branch, as planned by the San Francisco constitution-makers. It was no more than a makeshift. Neither the General Assembly nor the North Atlantic Treaty Organization and its sister institutions possess the qualifications required in a true executive. They may, with skill and good fortune, fill the gap for a short time, but they are inherently unsatisfactory. No student of government would be content with such a provisional arrangement on the national level; and if the United Nations is to be equal to its exalted task it must certainly not lower its technical standards in order to meet unexpected emergencies; on the contrary, it should make them more precise and more exacting.

Let us then put the Security Council, the General Assembly, and the regional organizations to one side for a few moments and concentrate on this problem of the executive branch of the United Nations. What work is there for it to do? And what kind of organ is needed to perform this work?

As to the first question, what is required of the executive branch, the Charter itself is quite explicit. What is required is "prompt and effective action for the maintenance of international peace and security." In order to enable its executive to function "promptly and effectively," the Charter even went to the length of providing it with an instrument of action in the form of a Military Staff Committee.

In answer to the second question, what kind of organ is needed, the Charter is equally explicit. It lays it down that the executive organ shall consist of not more than eleven members and that "it shall be so organized as to be able to function continuously." In order to be within call, prepared to perform what we may call this night watchman's function, every member of the executive must be available "at all times at the seat of the organization." Those familiar with the text of the Charter will have noticed that, in the above references and analysis of the relevant Articles in the Security Council Chapter, one point has been glossed over. The actual words used, in one sentence, in the description of what has been called the night watchman's function are: *"each member of the Security Council for this purpose shall be represented at all times at the seat of the organization."* Now there is a difficulty—not to say, contradiction—here which leaps to the eye of the student of political science. We are dealing with a body of night watchmen, formed to deal with emergencies and equipped for instant action. How can the individual night watchmen also be *representatives*—not representatives of the United Nations as a whole, but representatives of the separate members of the Security Council, the individual states of which it is composed? Obviously, if the night watchmen are to continue to be diplomats, if they are under the obligation to refer back constantly for instructions to the governments or chancelleries of their respective states, they will have to leave the fire ablaze until they receive further orders. But, in that event, they will no longer be members of a *team*. In other words, they will no longer be part of an executive body; they will be members of what, in the language of political science, is termed a *conference*. Instead of being associated with one another in a first person plural relationship—"we of the world's fire brigade"—each one will be tied to an official superior in his own particular state capital.

In such circumstances could any fire brigade function effectively or command confidence, least of all an international fire brigade?

This point, which is left obscure—one would not wish to say

deliberately glossed over—in Article 24 of the Charter, when it speaks of "prompt and effective action," is in reality one of the highest importance. The legislature of the United Nations is, very properly, a body of representatives drawn from the member states and, in a greater or lesser degree, that relationship must always continue. The Congress of the United States and the British House of Commons have developed traditions, habits, and institutional loyalties of their own: but behind them stand all the time the voters in their several constituencies to whom they have periodically to render account. Thus a parliamentary body can never become *organic* in the full sense of that word.

But the situation is different in the case of an executive body, which is, from the very nature of its work, a limited group, a team —numbering at the most eleven, and at the best, as we have seen, seven. The members of such a group must devote themselves wholly to their task and to one another. They must know one another intimately enough to be able to follow one another's mental processes. And in the case of a task so responsible, so *sacred*, as that of the safety of the civilized world, they must not only be a bond of brothers but also individually dedicated men.

Other qualifications are needed and they will shortly be mentioned; but what has just been said is the first and foremost requirement. *Dedication* is *essential*. It is essential for the conduct of the work itself. It is essential also in order to win, and to maintain, the confidence of the member peoples. If it is said by "experts in international organization" that such persons are not to be found, then the answer is that the doubters do not know where to look for them, or to recognize them when they cross their path. It is the dedicated people who make the wheels of the world go around. This is a task which calls for single-minded and wholehearted concentration, uninterrupted by considerations of personal prestige or "public relations." Perhaps the very fact that such men are entirely devoted to their tasks, paying little attention to external appearances, explains why the world's best workers are not always quickly recognized for what they are.

What other qualifications are needed in the executive team?

It must be representative in the sense that its members between them must represent, in a broad sense, the chief cultures and traditions of the world. They must not all be European, or all Asian, or all American, or all African, but must exemplify the best of each of these, so as to be a living symbol of "the equality of peoples" which, as has already been emphasized, is one of the great distinguishing marks of the present age, as compared with the period of the League of Nations.

That they must have experience of public life on the international level need hardly be added. Had they not earned their spurs in this field their names would never have come into question for this more responsible work. But it is not enough for them individually to have wide experience and tested judgment. They must have given proof of possessing the gift, or art, of social co-operation and of being proficient in practicing this on the international level. This is not only a high intellectual qualification; it is also a moral qualification. A man may be a genius, yet unable to function in a team. Anyone with experience of the international environment knows this. Clever men were always more plentiful at Geneva than good men; and it would be strange if the same were not true in the new international society in New York. This is not to say that the members of the United Nations Executive should be saints. This would be too much to ask. But the more saintliness there is in their joint composition, the better it will be for their work and for the world. And does not the word "saint" spring to the lips in connection with some, at least, of the members of the Combined Chiefs of Staff dealt with in an earlier chapter?

CHAPTER 71: *The Organization of Security without the Security Council*

IN the preceding chapters we have tried to make it clear that the principal defect of the present organization of the United Nations,

viewed from the constitutional angle, is that it is not provided
with one of the most essential elements in any government, a true
executive: and we have explained how this serious gap in its make-
up came about and how an attempt was made, both in the Covenant of the League of Nations and in the Charter of the United
Nations, to conceal this deficiency by the use of ambiguous and
misleading terms. We then proceeded to set forth briefly what
kind of body was required to fill this gap. At this stage of the
development of the United Nations, our treatment of this subject
can be no more than an outline sketch. To discuss it in detail on
the technical level, as its importance demands, would call for a
work devoted entirely to this problem. Let it only be said in passing, that, if nothing has been said on the relation between the
Executive—however it may be composed, and however its duties
may be defined—and the other United Nations organs, it is not
because that subject has been overlooked. It should be one of the
principal questions threshed out in the world-wide discussion
which must precede the Assembly debate on the revision of the
Charter in a few years' time.

Meanwhile let us prepare the ground for such a discussion by
surveying the developments which have come about in the structure of the United Nations since 1945 and considering where and
how the place might be found for the much-needed executive
body.

We observed in a previous chapter that the functions of the Security Council had been partly taken over by other organizations
of two kinds: firstly, by the General Assembly, and, secondly, by
the regional bodies set up under Article 51, or in other ways.

The first set of expedients were those to which the General
Assembly had recourse in the fall of 1950, a few months after the
occurrence of aggression in Korea, on the initiative of the United
States delegation. The proposals brought forward on that occasion, and adopted by an overwhelming majority of the members
of the General Assembly, involved four recommendations
designed to increase the effectiveness of the United Nations
action against aggression.

1. The calling of an emergency session of the General Assembly upon 24 hours notice, if the Security Council is prevented from acting upon a breach of the peace or an act of aggression. (Incidentally, this involves a delay of from 24 to 48 hours, which in some circumstances might be disastrous. What fire brigade could function under such a rule?)

2. The establishment by the Assembly of a security patrol, for immediate independent observation and reporting from any area where international conflict is threatened, upon the invitation and with the consent of the state to be visited (This provision has already been put into effect with good results, since a frontier dispute in a peculiarly delicate area in the Balkans was allayed by the prompt dispatch of a United Nations patrol from Salonika in August, 1952.)

3. A plan under which each member would designate within its own armed forces a United Nation unit or units, to be specially trained and equipped and continuously maintained for United Nation service: and the appointment of United Nations military advisers for the organization and training of such units.

4. The establishment by the Assembly of a Committee to study and report on means which the United Nations might use through collective action, including the use of armed forces, to carry out the principles and purposes of the Charter.

This last-named body was duly formed, under the name of the Collective Measures Committee, and began to work on its task, which was not concluded when the Assembly of 1950 adjourned or in the Assembly of 1951. It must be confessed that neither the Collective Measures Committee nor the other expedients mentioned above excited the interest or enlisted the world-wide support to which their objects should have entitled them. Equally disappointing has been the response of United Nations members other than the United States, whether by means of "specially maintained" military units or otherwise, to the call to member-nations to assist in resistance against the North Korean and Red Chinese aggression in Korea. Many reasons, of varying validity, may be assigned for this in the case of individual United Nations members. But the glaring fact remains that the total military contributions, some of them little more than token contributions, came from less than one third of the member nations and that the United Nations, with its imposing claims and its sixty-nations membership, has been placed in the humiliating position of carrying on military operations under stalemate conditions against the forces of two governmental organizations neither of them enjoying the advantage of official recognition by the majority of the world's governments.

What is the reason for this unsatisfactory state of things? Above and beyond all the particular reasons which may be given there is one general explanation which stands out. It is that, in the absence of a true United Nations executive, too much responsibility has been thrown upon a single government, the government of the United States, and that there are still many nations, particularly nonwhite nations, who have not yet brought themselves to trust the American government and people or to recognize that the central place on the political stage of the world is now occupied by a Great Power of a type different from that of its European predecessors and representing new principles and new standards of conduct in international relationships.

It is unreasonable to expect that the leaders of nations such as India or Indonesia or the Arab peoples or the peoples of Indo-China will acquire full confidence in the United States, or in the United Nations under American leadership, and convey that confidence to their peoples, until the equality of nations proclaimed by the United States has been manifested by some signal political act; and it is equally unreasonable—not to say, undignified—for much of the rest of the world to go on receiving large-scale material assistance from the United States while so many nations cannot bring themselves to entertain feelings of gratitude or sincere friendship and remain suspicious of the motives by which the policy of the United States government is inspired.

When a psychological situation of this kind occurs on the domestic scene, there is a recognized way of dealing with it. If a member, or a group of members, in an organization are "dragging their feet," the natural thing is for those who are charged with the conduct of affairs to find some way of giving those who lag behind a more responsible position in the organization. "Why not put him on the committee?" is a familiar refrain on such occasions. With tact and a sufficient amount of good will on both sides this expedient seldom fails; for it appeals to something deep down in the nature of man as a social being.

Cannot some stimulus of the same kind be applied to nations, and, in particular to the members of the United Nations?

The answer is that it not only can be applied but is being applied with remarkable and increasing success by the application of the regional principle: for the great advantage of that principle is that, by reducing international problems and responsibilities to dimensions which make a more direct appeal to the ordinary citizen, especially in a small state, it enlists in the service of international co-operation energies which are left dormant when the matters in question seem dim and distant, unrelated to the affairs and interests of his own particular country.

We have already encountered the regional principle several times. We saw how, in his Mobile speech Woodrow Wilson linked the idea of the solidarity of the New World with his own larger outlook. We saw also how the application of the regional principle in the Far East, through the Washington treaties, led to grievous failure owing to the lack of a general international framework, and how the Locarno agreements, also conceived on regional lines, proved abortive for the same reason. But Western statesmanship, warned by these examples, has in recent years given the regional principle a new lease of life by associating it with the United Nations Charter.

The postwar measures that have been taken in this connection concern three regions: the North Atlantic, Latin America, and the Far East. Other measures have been under contemplation in the Middle East: but they have not yet assumed definite shape. It is, however, not too early to say that the free world is in process of being divided up into a series of regions with autonomous organizations in varying stages of development, under the auspices and with the full knowledge and approval of the over-all United Nations.

Let us look in succession at the three regions in which organizations have actually been set up; for these developments are of greatest interest to the political scientist. By far the most advanced and detailed of these organizations is the North Atlantic Treaty Organization, known as NATO.

Regional organization in the North Atlantic area was a direct result of the action of the Soviet Government in bringing the whole of Eastern Europe under its control between 1945 and 1948, a process which culminated in the subjection of Czecho-Slovakia: all this was a violation of a number of treaties and agreements already noted in these pages, including the Charter of the United Nations and the Yalta "Declaration on Liberated Europe." It was also a reaction to the efforts of the Soviet Union to counteract the European Recovery Program initiated in the Marshall Plan and to the failure of the Four-Power control of Germany planned at Potsdam in 1945.

It was in these circumstances that the Western governments decided to make use of Article 51 of the Charter, which lays it down that:

> nothing in this Charter shall impair the inherent right of individual or collective self-defence if an armed attack occurs against a Member of the United Nations, until the Security Council has taken the measures necessary to maintain international peace and security.

It should be noted in passing that Article 51 in Chapter VII was used in preference to the immediately following Articles in Chapter VIII, which are specifically devoted to "Regional Arrangements." This choice was dictated by the fact that action under Chapter VIII requires authorization by the Security Council. As the "armed attack" by the Soviet Union has been directed against nations who have been deprived of the possibility of invoking the aid of the Charter in their self-defense, and as the members of the North Atlantic Treaty Organization, although subjected to *threats* of aggression, have none of them been subject to actual "armed attack," it could be argued that the use of Article 51 in this connection would be strengthened if it were confirmed by an Advisory Opinion of the International Court of Justice. However, neither the Executive nor the Senate of the United States has felt any doubt as to the rightful application of Article 51.

This was made clear in the Resolution introduced into the Senate by Senator Vandenberg June 11, 1948 and accepted by sixty-four votes to four. The Vandenberg Resolution declared the determination of the American people to "exercise the right of individual or collective self-defense" under Article 51. It went on to foreshadow the "progressive development of regional and other collective arrangements" and recommended that the United States should be associated with "such other regional and collective arrangements as are based on continuous and effective self-help and mutual aid."

This language is re-echoed in the North Atlantic Treaty itself, which was signed in Washington on April 4, 1949 and came into force, after ratification by all its signatories, on August 24 of the same year. In the Preamble the signatories

"re-affirm their faith in the purposes and principles of the Charter of the United Nations" and declare their resolve "to unite their efforts for collective defence and for the preservation of peace and security:" and in Article 3 the Parties pledge themselves "by means of continuous and effective self-help and mutual aid" to "maintain and develop their individual and corporate capacity to resist armed attack."

But the special interest of the Treaty from the standpoint of the organization of the United Nations lies in Article 9. That Article reads as follows:

The Parties hereby establish a council on which each of them shall be represented, to consider measures concerning the implementation of this Treaty. The Council shall be so organized as to be able to meet promptly at any time. The Council shall set up such subsidiary bodies as may be necessary; in particular it shall establish immediately a defense committee which shall recommend measures for the implementation of Articles 3 and 5 (Article 5 contains the pledge of mutual assistance.)

In the few short years since 1949 the NATO Council has developed rapidly. In its early form it consisted of the foreign ministers, the defense ministers, and the finance ministers of the twelve (later fourteen) countries, with deputies qualified to act in their absence. Beneath this over-all body there were four other organs —a Military Committee, a Defense Production Board, a Financial and Economic Board and a Planning Board for Ocean Shipping. For those who remember World War I these sub-divisions had a familiar ring; but what was new and, so far as Europe is concerned, epoch-making was their appearance in time of nominal peace.

After the Lisbon Conference of February, 1952, there was a general reorganization. A "Permanent Organization" was set up of which the Deputies became a regular part, under the title of Permanent Representatives. They continue to act as representatives of national governments, but they are now regarded as "the Council itself in permanent session." The Defense Production Board and the Financial and Economic Board were merged with the Permanent Organization and these and other bodies, such as the Standing Military Group in Washington, are served by common staffs. The Vice-Chairman of the Council assumed the additional post of Secretary-General and was thus brought into direct touch, on the one hand with the delegations of the fourteen nations on the Council, and, on the other, with the staff of the Permanent Organization. This pivotal post is at present occupied by Lord Ismay, the close wartime associate of Mr. Winston Churchill. The American Permanent Representative is Mr. William H. Draper, who is the nearest counterpart in the civil realm to the Supreme Commander. The power that he can exercise, however, is derived not so much from his place in the official NATO set-up as from his key position in the planning and distribution of the economic aid supplied by the United States government.

The Military Committee already mentioned consists of the chiefs of staff of the member states. It has not, like the other boards, been merged in the Permanent Organization, but retains its separate identity in Paris. Beneath it, in the official hierarchy, there is a Committee in Washington composed of military representatives of the fourteen States, and a "Standing Group" composed of one member each from the chiefs of staff of France, Great Britain and the United States.

Beneath this "Standing Group" there is the Supreme Headquarters of the Allied Powers in Europe (SHAPE), itself subdivided into a series of local commands covering land, sea, and air forces.

It is unnecessary to carry this description further—all the more so, as it is subject to constant modification. But its rapid flowering, in contrast with the sterility of the military clauses of the security chapter of the Charter, shows that the instinct of the statesmen who framed the 1949 Treaty was sound and that the regional principle contains the seed of life.

Let us turn now to another region: that covered by the Organization of American States (O.A.S.).

The idea of an organization for inter-American co-operation goes back to the "Treaty of Perpetual Union, League and Confederation" signed in 1826 by delegates of Central and South American countries who met at the invitation of Simon Bolivar in a congress at Panama. No practical steps were taken to implement it however, until 1890, when the eighteen countries attending the First International Conference of American States in Washington formed the International Union of American Republics "for the prompt collection and distribution of commercial information." From this beginning the complex of agencies and institutions known as the "inter-American system" was developed.

The Ninth International Conference of American States, held in Bogota in 1948, adopted the Charter of the Organization of

American States (O.A.S.) in its present form. This organization carries on its work through three sorts of institutions: the Conference, the Council with the Pan-American Union (situated in Washington as its General Secretariat), and a number of specialized organizations.

The *Conference* meets every five years at a time fixed by the Council, all member states having the right to be represented with one vote each. The *Council* is the permanent executive organ of the organization, and is composed of a representative of each member state. It is the body authorized to act, pending a meeting of foreign ministers, as the organ through which governments carry out consultations and take decisions (including the imposition of sanctions) under the Inter-American Treaty of Reciprocal Assistance.

Under the Council there are three more specialized bodies: the Inter-American Economic and Social Council, the Inter-American Council of Jurists, and the Inter-American Cultural Council. Thus it is in its way, a miniature United Nations. But the Charter of the O.A.S. is careful to avoid any possibility of conflict between the two organizations by laying it down that it is its duty to "fulfill its regional obligations under the Charter of the United Nations."

Provision is also made in the O.A.S. Charter for Meetings of Consultation of Ministers of Foreign Affairs, which are held when necessary "in order to consider problems of an urgent nature and of common interest to the American States and to serve as an Organ of Consultation."

Thus action is provided for on three levels: the Conference, which may hold special meetings between its quinquennial sessions; the Meetings of Consultation of Foreign Ministers; and the Council proper, the regular members of which are of ambassadorial rank.

We come now to the third and last of the regional organizations which have hitherto taken shape—that in the Security Treaty between the United States, Australia and New Zealand which was signed at San Francisco on September 1, 1951. Although there were only three signatory states to this treaty, it was explicitly drawn up with a view to its becoming the nucleus for a more comprehensive defense organization in the Far Eastern area.

Following the model of the North-Atlantic and Latin-American arrangements, this treaty establishes a Council of Foreign Ministers, or their Deputies, "to consider matters concerning the implementation" of the treaty, and "so organized as to be able to meet at any time." Article 5 is even more revealing in its indications. "Pending the development of a more comprehensive system of regional security in the Pacific area," it runs, "and the development by the United Nations of more effective means to maintain international peace and security, the Council established by Article 7 is authorized to maintain a consultative relationship with states, regional organizations, associations of states, or other authorities in the Pacific area in a position to further the purpose of this treaty and so to contribute to the security of that area."

The framers of the treaty evidently had it in view that all the states in the area which are members of the United Nations would eventually enter into this partnership. When one reflects that this region contains more than half the population of the globe, that it extends from the Siberian frontier to the South Pacific and includes two of the great nations of the world—the Indians and the Chinese—the ambitious nature of its design is manifest. But, apart from all the secondary difficulties standing in the way of its realization, there is one major obstacle, to which attention has already been drawn—the lack of sufficient *confidence* between East and West.

Confidence is also the key to the organization of an adequate system of security in the Middle East and Africa. That region is passing through a stage of rapid "de-colonization," and it would be courting failure to plan its defenses through an arrangement confined to the European Powers which still exercise responsibilities there. Equally foolish would it be to imagine that their co-operation and experience could be dispensed with. The West, and especially the United States, has a large part to play in Africa, more particularly in Africa south of the Sahara. We cannot here touch on the internal problems of the various territories in this vast region, but defense is a common problem which should bring them all round the same table and break down the barriers which still divide Liberia from the Gold Coast and Nigeria, the Congo from Angola and Mozambique, and South Africa from Madagascar. The hardened white official at grips with rinderpest or cocoa blight may dismiss such prospects with a shrug of the shoulders. But let him look back fifty years and recall how narrow was the perspective of those who framed the policies of those days. The United Nations may have to wait a generation or more before the confidence of the Arab world, which Bayard Dodge and other American pioneers of education had succeeded in winning, is retrieved and before the American people realizes the magnitude of the process of democratization which is already being carried through in some of the countries of Central Africa. But the day will come when the peoples of that region, having achieved a cultural independence matching their political emancipation, will be among the chief defenders of the United Nations Charter.

There is one expanse of territory which has so far been left out of this survey—the lands east and north of the North Atlantic area and north of the countries included in the design of the pact between the United States, Australia, and New Zealand. This is the Heartland of Mackinder, known today as the region behind the Iron Curtain.

Behind this Iron Curtain there are two kinds of peoples, some who have grown up as part of Western civilization and are *temporarily* enslaved and others, the permanent population of that region, who are still at an early stage of their social and political development. Today, it is the most backward region of the globe, in spite of its recent technological exploits. These have produced a veneer of "progress," the promoters and misguided Western advocates of which glory in destroying the dignity of man while trying to compete with his Creator.

The political problem which this region presents to Western statesmanship, and to American statesmanship in particular, is evident enough today to the Western peoples. Would that it had been recognized sooner instead of being obscured by wishful thinking and sterile "ideological" controversies! There have been many occasions since the unfortunate events of October, 1917, when effective action could have been taken and it is only fair to recall that the Swiss, with their long experience of free institutions and their well-trained judgment, showed unerring insight in this matter. On the day when the Soviet delegation was admitted to the League of Nations, one could sense an atmosphere of intense fear mingled with indignation. The Swiss people wondered whether that day was not the funeral of peace and freedom for the world. As matters now are, the problem is much more difficult and complicated to deal with, but effective solutions could still be found. In the battle of principles which lies before us, the details are incalculable and the timing uncertain. But, if the Western peoples remain true to themselves and have moral courage, the victory of good government and peace can be won.

CHAPTER 72: *A Blue Print of the Eventual Executive*

IN Chapter 70 we saw what kind of an executive the United Nations needs—a body of some seven dedicated and experienced men constituting a living example of the equality of peoples. But we have as yet said nothing as to how such a body could be brought into existence.

Clearly, the General Assembly is not a body well suited for such a task. There is too great a disproportion between its voting system and the responsibilities which lie behind it. It is good that the small states should be well represented there and no lover of democracy would wish to stifle any voice that is the authentic expression of a nation, however limited in numbers. But a body on which nine-tenths of the financial burden is borne by one-tenth of the members and all have a vote of equal value is clearly not qualified to act as an electing body. That its part in the election of the judges of the International Court of Justice has been carried through as well as it has is due to the fact that its choice has been limited by the panel system devised by Elihu Root. What is needed is some arrangement which, while giving due weight to the smaller states, will take into account the degree of responsibility which they and their more powerful colleagues are prepared to take upon their shoulders.

A system based on considerations of this kind was not in sight in 1945 and the San Francisco Conference cannot therefore be criticized for not considering any advance along that line. But the situation is very different today. The defense systems described in the preceding chapter do, in fact, establish *degrees of responsibility*, even to the extent of excluding states who are unwilling to partake in any responsibility whatsoever. Thus the three regional "councils" which have already been formed are bodies composed of tried and experienced statesmen who are accustomed to work together and to trust one another. They are, in fact, the very type of men who might well be entrusted with executive responsibilty under the United Nations.

This is not, however, the proposition which is being put forward. For the time for such a choice has clearly not yet arrived. What *is* being suggested for consideration by all who are concerned with the future of the United Nations is that, *if and when* the regional design has been worked out in reasonable fullness in the four regions dealt with in the last chapter—the North Atlantic, Latin America, Eastern Asia and Australasia, and the Middle East and Africa—a joint body composed of the Councils of these four regions and of the Heartland region, if and when it is constituted, would be a suitable body for choosing the members of a true executive of the United Nations. Such a body would be composed of the most experienced statesmen in the world. It would be thoroughly representative of the diversity of peoples and of cultures. Its members would be well aware of the qualifications needed for membership of such an executive post and it would be natural to suppose that their choice would fall upon some at least of those who were, or had been, members of the Councils of their respective regions.

Before leaving this subject, let us consider it briefly from the angle of political science. There are three kinds of constitutional executives functioning in the world of states today. There is the executive responsible to a parliament, the British and French type. This is ruled out from consideration by the nature of the General Assembly, which it is not proposed to change, owing to the value inherent in its diversity. There is the executive elected directly by the people, in accordance with the doctrine of the Separation of Powers. This is the system adopted in the United States Constitution. It has great merits, but it is clearly inapplicable to the United Nations. There remains the third system, that of the Swiss Constitution of 1848, as it exists after the experience of over a century. Until very recently, this system was unique in the world, but the people of Uruguay have lately paid the Swiss the high compliment of adopting it for use in their own country.

The relevant articles of the Swiss Constitution, Articles 95 and 96, are as follows:

> The supreme directing and executive authority of the Confederation is exercised by a federal council composed of seven members.
>
> Members of the Federal Council are appointed for four years by the councils (i.e. the two legislative bodies of the country, the National Council and the Council of States, roughly comparable to the U.S. House of Representatives and the U.S. Senate) in joint session, and are chosen from among all Swiss citizens eligible for the National Council: no more than one member of the Federal Council may, however, be chosen in the same canton. The Federal Council is completely renewed after every renewal of the National Council. Vacancies arising during the period of four years are filled at the next meeting of the Federal Assembly, for the remainder of the period of office.

But the bare letter gives a very inadequate account of the Swiss executive as it has come to be after a century's working.

Although in theory it is renewed every four years, in actual fact the members generally retain their position during the rest of their working lives. In other words, they cease to be acting members of their respective political parties and become more like what are known in the United States as elder statesmen, but Elder Statesmen still at a desk. Thus their mentality resembles rather that of civil servants than of parliamentarians—but of civil servants of a very elevated type. That they are universally respected in the country need hardly be stated. This respect is enhanced by the fact that, at any given moment, one of their number occupies the position of president and another that of vice-president of the Swiss Confederation. These nominations are made by the Federal Assembly and customarily rotate among the members of the Federal Council.

We cannot, within these limits, dwell upon the powers and duties of the Federal Council, which are enumerated in Article 102. Article 103 is, however, important from the angle of the United Nations. "The business of the Federal Council is distributed among its members by departments. Decisions emanate from the Federal Council as a single authority."

The members of the United Nations Executive would, of course, carry on their duties at the headquarters of the U.N. Their regular presence there would be one of the chief advantages brought about by the creation of their position. This would bring them into immediate relationship with the secretary-general. As has already been said, this raises issues regarding the relationship of the new executive to the existing organization with which it is not desired to deal in these pages. But it seems relevant to recall one significant new development which has taken place in the North Atlantic Organization, where the vice-president of the Council also holds the position of secretary-general and is thus directly responsible for the detailed work of the organization.

It would not be right to leave this subject without pointing out how unsatisfactory is the position of the U.N. Secretariat at the present time and how ungrateful is the task of those of its members who are dedicated men and women. A body of 4,000 officials without any ministerial head would constitute a difficult problem under any circumstances. But when the body in question is international and appointments in it are subject to pressures of many different kinds, and when some of the appointees represent governments which, to say the least, are not wholly loyal to the principles and purposes of the organization, the problem is much intensified. This is a matter which deserves much closer consideration than it has yet received before it comes, as it is bound to come, before the Revising Assembly.

CHAPTER 73: *The Judicial Branch*

IN the preceding chapters we have seen that the United Nations organization already possesses a Legislature and we have provided it with an Executive—at least in prospect. What of the third branch of government—the Judicial?

This might seem to be the simplest part of our task! For is it not the purpose of the United Nations to place mankind under the Rule of Law? And cannot that be attained, in the larger constitutional system which we have been outlining, through arrangements similar to those which have so well served the people of the United States? Is there not an International Court of Justice already in existence and could not its powers be extended and adapted to resemble those of the Supreme Court of the United States, the trusted guardian of the United States Constitution?

But the problem is not so simple as that. The best evidence of this is the fact that, although the World Court, as it has come to be called, has existed, in one form under the League of Nations and in another under the United Nations, for over thirty years, it is still far from having acquired the authority which should belong to it in a true constitutional system.

Why is it that the World Court has thus remained in the background, not only in the actual conduct of world affairs but also in public opinion, in men's thinking about the problem of the organization of peace? Why, for instance, has so much attention and effort been devoted to other problems, such as armaments, economic questions, and dependent territories, rather than to what might seem to be the overriding need for strengthening the authority of the Court as the symbol and chief bulwark of the supremacy of law over brute force.

There have been two chief reasons for this. The first is that the predominance of the Great Powers has constantly hampered the work of the Court. There is indeed a standing contradiction between the two concepts—between the concept of a "Great Power" and the concept of a "Rule of Law." From the time when State Sovereignty became an accepted doctrine in the European diplomatic system, a Great Power was a Power *above the law*, though this was sometimes obscured by the hypocritical pretense that what the Great Powers agreed upon, even if it did violence to weaker states, *was* the law. Statesmen even used the term "the Public Law of Europe."

In the constitutional development of individual European countries this issue had to be fought out between the Executive and the Judiciary and was only settled when the latter became established as an independent branch of the government. There are, of course, many countries in the world where this has not yet been achieved. Indeed, it is conceivable that, in spite of the precautions taken by Elihu Root in framing the arrangements for the choice of candidates and the election of judges, the World Court itself might sink into becoming subordinate to the other branches of the Government. The battle for judicial independence is never won. It needs to be carried on generation after generation. There is no part of the governmental process to which the maxim, "eternal vigilance is the price of liberty," needs to be more constantly applied. Even in the short history of the World Court this could be illustrated by concrete examples.

The second reason why the World Court has failed to acquire the authority which is its due is that there are important differences between the problems facing the Court on the world level and the problems facing the supreme judicature on the national level. Until these are recognized and met, the Rule of Law on the world level will remain little more than a form of words.

In discussing the thought of Woodrow Wilson and Elihu Root, we found it necessary to break up the subject into two divisions, which we termed "the Statesmen's Court" and the "Jurists' Court," but we made no effort to relate the one to the other. At that stage of the argument, there was nothing to be done but to leave the subject in the air. In taking it up again at this final stage let us begin by examining these two realms—that of the jurist, and what we have called that of the statesman—on the national level. It will be simplest to take the case of the United States.

In the United States the needs of justice are well supplied. There are indeed two parallel systems for the administration of justice, one on the federal and another on the state level. With this duality we are not here concerned, since, whatever the world authority may turn out to be, it is not likely to be a federal system in the American sense. Let us confine ourselves then to the institutions of the central government.

In that government we find three agencies which are in, or close to, the realm of justice; the federal courts with the Supreme Court at their apex, the Federal Mediation and Conciliation Service, an independent government agency, and the Department of Justice, headed by the attorney general. These agencies are not peculiar to the United States. They exist in somewhat similar form, in Great Britain and other countries.

In the above enumeration no account has been taken of the administrative agencies which exercise judicial or quasi-judicial functions in limited fields. These have developed greatly in recent years, both in the United States and in Great Britain owing to the wide extension of legislative activity in the social and economic fields. Left to themselves, they might have developed a "new tyranny" on Star Chamber Lines. However, the need for safeguards to ensure that they maintain the canons of the judicial process is now generally recognized. In France this principle has been institutionalized through a special body, the "Council of State" (*Con-*

256

seil d'État) which deals with cases in which there is a conflict of jurisdiction between the administrative system in that country and the ordinary courts of justice.

It is not necessary to deal with this matter further here, since the question of creating permanent institutions of this kind on the international level has not yet become an issue. Nevertheless, students of world affairs should keep watch on developments in this field, since, in a world in which the Great Power tradition is still powerful, there is always a danger that arbitrary methods may creep in.

Let us come back now to the four agencies on the national level. What are their respective functions? And how are they related to one another?

Let us summarize very briefly the part they play in the American system.

The courts of law in the United States, as in other modern states, perform two functions. They decide issues affecting individual citizens or groups of citizens, both in the civil and the criminal realm; and they watch over the maintenance of the Constitution. The Federal Mediation and Conciliation Service deals with matters which, for one reason or another, it is considered better to submit to treatment which is not strictly judicial. The Ministry of Justice is a body concerned with the machinery of judicial administration including, in some countries, but not in the United States, the appointment of judges, while the attorney general also plays the part of legal adviser to the government, as individual attorneys act for private citizens.

Now let us look at these agencies as they have hitherto functioned on the international level.

With the World Court we are already familiar. We saw how it was brought into existence, through the efforts of Elihu Root and others, and how its jurisdiction was circumscribed. It has no criminal jurisdiction whatsoever; an attempt to remedy this deficiency was made by certain states in the Nurenberg trials, but, whatever may be thought of the machinery adopted in them for dealing with crimes connected with the outbreak and conduct of warfare, it has not so far been brought into relation with the

United Nations Charter and thus concerns only a limited number of members of the United Nations.

As regards the civil sphere, to which the World Courts' jurisdiction is limited, it can only hand down decisions or judgments on disputes which both parties have agreed to submit to it. As the record of the last thirty years has shown, such disputes are generally not of the kind which involves an immediate danger of a breach of the peace.

Thus, at the first sight, the World Court might seem to have little direct bearing on the organization of world peace.

There is one respect however, in which the World Court goes beyond the Supreme Court of the United States and the courts of most of the states. As we saw earlier, it is authorized to give *advisory opinions* "on any legal question at the request of whatever body may be authorized by or in accordance with the Charter of the United Nations to make such a request." Article 96 of the Charter provides that "the General Assembly or the Security Council"—let us say the Legislature and the Executive—"may request the International Court of Justice to give an advisory opinion on any legal question" and that "other organs of the United Nations and specialized agencies may at any time be authorized by the General Assembly to do so."

Some use has been made of this provision, both under the League of Nations and under the United Nations, but its possibilities have so far not been fully explored or realized by public opinion.

The United States Mediation and Conciliation Service finds its parallel in what we called the "Statesmen's Court." In using that phrase we were falling in with the attitude of Woodrow Wilson, who preferred to make a clean cut between a full-dress court of international justice and the essentially political machinery of the League of Nations. But once we bring mediation and conciliation into the picture, it is necessary to cover the whole field of procedures available for settling disputes on the international level. These include *arbitration* as well as mediation and conciliation.

Arbitration is a familiar word in the field of international relations and it was, in fact, the earliest method of dealing with disputes between states to be institutionalized. The Hague Conference of 1899 established the Permanent Court of Arbitration at The Hague, and this is still in existence side by side with the International Court of Justice or World Court. Already before that time arbitration had an honorable place in the history of American foreign relations. It was through the method of arbitration that the boundary line between the United States and Canada was fixed by the Jay Treaty of 1794 and it was by using the same method that the vexatious dispute between the United States and Great Britain arising out of the depredations of the cruiser *Alabama* was settled in 1871.

But the Permanent Court of Arbitration, as we have already observed, is not a court in the usual sense of that term. It is only a *framework for a court—a permanent* framework for *temporary* tribunals—that is to say, for tribunals brought into existence from time to time, *ad hoc*, to deal with particular disputes. This framework consists of a body of rules, a list of suitable arbitrators available for the parties to a dispute to choose from, and a permanent office or secretariat for the keeping of archives and the receipt of applications and other correspondence.

In the field of American domestic politics arbitration is a much more controversial term in the ears of many American citizens, particularly when it is preceded by the adjective "compulsory." It is worth while pausing to ask why this should be so. It would seem to be due to two reasons. First, because the term has come to be associated with the issue between management and labor in the never-ending struggle in the economic system over rates of pay and conditions of work. In that struggle labor started out at a decided disadvantage; it was dissatisfied with the existing position, with what diplomats call the *status quo,* and was constantly seeking to change it in its favor; it was therefore opposed to action by bodies of recognized arbitrators which might lay down principles, as they thought, prematurely, and so tend to freeze situations which they preferred to keep fluid with a view to further advances in the future. This situation has been considerably modified in recent years, but the whole subject still remains charged with controversy. It is only mentioned here in order to bring out the analogy with a similar situation on the international level. Here, too, there are important social groups—notably those which have previously been, or still are, under colonial rule—who feel that they are starting out from a position of inferiority which they are determined to improve. They are therefore not inclined to allow bodies of judges or arbitrators to lay down fixed standards at this early stage of their advance, except on matters of very general principle, such as are already laid down in the Preamble of the Charter.

A second reason why the word arbitration has to some extent lost repute lies in the doubt which surrounds the meaning of the term. For it has both a broad and a narrow meaning. In its broad meaning it is applied to any kind of settlement of a dispute between states reached otherwise than by an appeal to force. It is true that the rules laid down by the professional international body concerned with these matters, the Institute of International Law, lay it down that "international arbitration has for its object the settlement of differences between states by *judges* of their own choice and *on the basis of respect for law*." But there is an ambiguity in the words "respect for law," which has never been cleared up. Indeed, this issue is still being debated in the International Law Commission, an advisory committee of experts appointed by the United Nations, which concluded its fourth session in Geneva in August, 1952. This meeting brought to light a deep-lying difference of opinion between two of its eminent members. One of them, the special Rapporteur on Arbitral Procedure, had proposed, in a draft convention drawn up for his colleagues, that an arbitral tribunal should be free to act as a conciliator by agreement between the parties in cases where "the positive law was silent or obscure." Against this another member argued that to permit an arbitration tribunal to serve as a conciliator was a purely *political* way of settling a dispute. If the parties agreed that the dispute should be settled that way, on the basis of political considerations, they had only to refer it to a conciliation commission.

But a settlement on that basis was alien to the whole character of international arbitration.

However this may be, the Permanent Court of Arbitration remains and, though not much use has been made of it in recent years, it performs two useful functions. One is to supply machinery for providing candidates for the post of judge of the International Court of Justice, a task which, as all experience shows, could not safely be left to the individual governments; and the other is to preserve a reasonable degree of flexibility in the arrangements for dealing with disputes between states; for, as a high authority has observed, "there will continue to be cases which states, for one reason or another, prefer to take to arbitration and what matters is that disputes should be settled, not that they should be settled by a particular procedure."

On this one further observation may be made. It is not always necessary, or even desirable, that disputes between states should be "settled," when the necessary atmosphere for a friendly settlement between the parties is not forthcoming. What *is* necessary is to ensure that the continuance of a dispute should involve, in the language of the Charter, no "threat to the peace, breach of the peace, or act of aggression." When a dispute is stagnant, it may be the wiser, or, at least, the less unsatisfactory, course to let it lie until circumstances have changed. Here we are in the realm of the unpredictable, where even the most experienced observers of the international scene may make different estimates. But it is the part of wisdom to leave open a loop-hole for the healing work of time rather than to drag one or more unwilling litigants into court when no danger to the public peace is to be feared.

But it is time to pick up the thread of our argument.

What is there on the international level corresponding to the United States Department of Justice? To this there is no single answer. The functions are divided between the Legal Department of the United Nations Secretariat and the office of the Registrar of the International Court of Justice. Of these two bodies the former has, at any rate hitherto, been considerably the more important. This is due to the reluctance of the Great Powers to use the machinery of the court to clear up difficulties which come up in the Security Council and also to a lesser extent in the Assembly. They were thus led to consult the legal authorities in the secretariat. This was no doubt a convenient practice, as compared with a request for an advisory opinion from the distant court. But it is open to question whether it was wise to lay a responsibility of this kind in regard to difficult issues upon administrative officials lacking the independence of the judicial branch.

As for the attorney-general, his opposite numbers on the international level are the legal advisers of the individual states. The legal advisers of the Great Powers played a large part in the history of the League of Nations and are still important in the United Nations. Their weight should diminish automatically as the Great Power concept sinks into the background and all the members of the General Assembly share equally in the judicial approach.

Let us now apply the results of the foregoing survey to the judicial branch of the United Nations as it might be after the forthcoming revision of the Charter.

It is clear that the new executive would have "primary responsibilities for the maintenance of international peace and security." As has been already argued, only a body of this type could effectively provide for the security of member nations and lift the burden of fear and anxiety which is at present hanging over the world, and will continue to do so in this age of "weapons of mass destruction" until confidence in international institutions both political and juridical has been built up.

But how far should the new Executive be related to the other organs of the United Nations and how far should its authority extend?

A good deal more light will be thrown on these questions in the next two or three years prior to the Revising Assembly, since during that time the General Assembly will be put on its mettle in dealing with issues which it was expected at San Francisco would fall within the scope of the Security Council. Generally speaking, we may say that the more responsibility the General Assembly is ready to assume in covering the ground assigned to the Security

Council in the Charter, the better it will be for the world and the sooner the traces of the old power-political system will disappear. Thus the General Assembly should normally take charge of the "Pacific Settlement of Disputes" under chapter 6 of the Charter—that is to say, where no breach of the peace or of general security has occurred or is threatened. But it would naturally do so in close association with the Executive and either body would be free to appoint fact-finding or other commissions or individual negotiators as it thought fit. It should not be necessary to delimit the respective fields of the two bodies provided the "primary responsibility" of the Executive to maintain or restore international peace and security is recognized and observed.

The Executive would as a matter of course remain in the closest touch with the General Assembly. This would be facilitated by its regular presence at the headquarters of the United Nations. Article 24, paragraph 3 requires the Security Council to "submit annual, and when necessary, special reports to the General Assembly for its consideration." It might be well to provide that the regular reports should, if possible, be monthly, and also to institute the practice of a weekly broadcast and televised talk. This would have the double advantage of enabling the members of the Executive, in their individual and corporate capacities, to become known to the peoples of the member nations all over the world and to emphasize their corporate solidarity and their unity of outlook and purpose. As for the question of voting, which has caused so much trouble in the short history of the United Nations, it would no longer arise. The Executive would be a cabinet and cabinets *do not take votes.* Instead, they *exchange opinions,* knowing well that, after exchanging opinions, no matter how difficult the question at issue, they *must* arrive at a common decision for which they must take collective responsibility. If one can put in a single sentence the trouble that mankind has been suffering from, it is the lack of an over-all body prepared to take collective responsibility for the condition of the world.

What of the relations between the Executive and the General Assembly on the one hand and the Judiciary on the other?

We have already partly answered that question.

The International Court of Justice should continue to exercise its present powers and no attempt should be made to extend them by revising the statute. The present arrangements are flexible enough to enable states which wish to make a fuller use of the judicial process to do so, either by special agreements among themselves to cover particular classes of cases in the future or by *ad hoc* arrangements. It will take some time for the transformation from the old sovereign-ridden international law to become law for the peoples of the United Nations in the true sense and be recognized as such. In due time, we may feel sure, the Court will produce spokesmen who will do for it, and for the civilized world, what John Marshall did for the Supreme Court of the United States. But this process cannot be hastened. There is great virtue in right timing, and this is particularly true of the interpretation of a document like the United Nations Charter, some clauses of which are open to different and indeed almost contradictory interpretations.

In the meantime, the Executive, the General Assembly, and the other organs of the United Nations should resort habitually to the Court for advisory opinions on matters of principle arising in the course of their work, instead of trying to build up an independent jurisprudence through their own experts, at the expense of the unity of the United Nations. This is a matter on which both the General Assembly and the Economic and Social Council should keep vigilant watch. There is a very great difference between the Rule of Law and the rule of office regulations. The struggle to "judicialize" administrative law in the United States and Great Britain will inevitably be transferred to the United Nations, where the officials of the central organization and the specialized agencies are at present working under conditions largely withdrawn from popular control. This is another facet of the problem examined in a preceding chapter—the supposed incompatibility between large-scale government and the democratic process. There is no one patent solution for this problem, but in present-day conditions it can certainly be kept under constant control and the democratic nations can be trusted to produce statesmen who will take the lead in doing so.

This is a very particular responsibility of the American people, not only because the headquarters and central institutions of the United Nations are on American soil, but also because of the active public spirit and alertness of the American community. If only a small part of the attention which the American public now so actively and conscientiously bestows on domestic politics was devoted to the affairs of the United Nations, of which the American taxpayer bears one third of the cost, the atmosphere of uncertainty and frustration which pervades at least parts of that institution would soon be swept away and would be replaced by the confidence and vigor which Americans know so well how to infuse; this would benefit the United States as well as the rest of the world. Until this has happened, the General Assembly and the other United Nations organs will be like ships becalmed in a fog, while the enemy makes use of the general inactivity and discouragement to press on with his disintegrating work without and within the organization. Happily the year of the Revising Assembly draws near; for, to those who watched the rise and fall of the League of Nations, symptoms of a parallel decline in the United Nations are only too evident.

We have left to the last what has hitherto been considered the most difficult problem of all in international relations, the problem usually described by such names as "changing the *status quo*," "the reconsideration of treaties which have become inapplicable," or "peaceful change."

To realize the nature and dimensions of this problem one need only look at a political map of the world as it was fifty years ago and compare it with the political map today, and then reflect on what, in the natural course of social change, that map is likely to show fifty years hence.

The political changes of the last fifty years have been brought about mostly by, or as a result of, two world wars, or, in other words, by revolution and force rather than by co-operation and consent. That the necessary political changes of the next fifty years should be brought about in the same way is a prospect both terrifying and paralyzing. But how else then can they be accomplished under the Rule of Law?

There seems to be only one answer. They must be brought about by *the force of public opinion*—the public opinion of free peoples, acting through their forum and meeting place, the General Assembly of the United Nations. That is why it is so necessary that the General Assembly should cease to be a collection of rival "blocks," contending for elected seats on the Security Council and for other marks of distinction and should take on its true character, which Woodrow Wilson foretold, that of expressing "the organized opinion of mankind."

There are situations in the world today which are manifestly contrary to the "fundamental human rights," "the dignity and worth of the human person," "the equal rights of men and women and of nations large and small" which the "members of the United Nations" have subscribed to as embodying their guiding rules in the conduct of public affairs. How could such situations be remedied?

If they involved "the existence of any threat to the peace, breach of the peace, or act of aggression," they would fall within the sphere of the Executive, which would take measures at its discretion, reporting to the General Assembly at each stage of its action, as in the case of a breach of the Atomic Energy Convention.

But some of the most intractable of these situations might well involve no danger, except of an indirect kind, to the general peace. Some day, no doubt, the World Court will hand down a ruling giving an interpretation of Article 39 of the Charter, from which the above words are taken. But when the Executive has had no authorization from the Court to take action under this article, there is nothing left to do except to bring to bear upon the situation the force of world public opinion acting through the General Assembly. That is the kind of appeal which Jefferson had in mind when, in immortal language, he urged that those who took the momentous step of declaring the independence of the United States should show "a decent respect to the opinions of mankind."

The United Nations Charter

Today, the champions of freedom have a parliament to appeal to, the most universal and the most representative that the world has ever seen. Is it likely that, if the general sense of mankind is placed on record not once but over several years, in declaring that a contradiction exists between the Charter and the acts of a particular government, that government will hold indefinitely to its course? If so, it will be hardening its heart and cutting itself off from the fellowship of the family of nations. Sooner or later uncomfortable situations of that kind become untenable.

Thus, if the people of the United States desire to use their great power constitutionally and through persuasion, rather than by the exercise of the force at their command in the traditional power-political manner, they should spare no effort to unite the nations of the free world upon a positive program based upon the principles of the Charter and to convince the other nations of the purity and sincerity of their motives, which their enemies are persistently impugning. If the rest of the world could see the people of the United States as they truly are, the future of the United Nations under American leadership would be assured and the peace of the world safeguarded for as far ahead as statesmen can see. It is not simply a pleasant form of words but sober truth to say that an understanding of the United States is the world's best insurance for peace.

But what, the reader may ask, of the Soviet Union? How can the United Nations make progress with this constant drag upon its wheels? And how can we look forward to a rosy future for the world when a gang of murderers and torturers holds so large a part of humanity under its heel?

One would not presume to give a definite answer to this question, into which so many uncertain factors enter, especially as regards the immediate future. But there are some things which seem clear.

One is that in fifty years' time—and this is a very generous reckoning—the Soviet Union will be a historic memory, like the blood-soaked empires of other conquerors who have ruled over the Russian steppes, and the peoples now under Soviet rule will have achieved freedom and independence under the terms of the Charter. The frontier between freedom and slavery which runs through Asia today is, in the eye of the historian, as temporary as many other lines drawn by rulers ignorant of the forces which determine the life of mankind.

Another thing which is clear—as it was clear five years ago to so levelheaded an observer of world affairs as the late Senator Vandenberg—is that the present widespread discouragement about the future of the United Nations is quite unjustified. The United Nations has been hampered at every stage of its progress by the treacherous hostility of the Soviet Union. During the time of weakness following an overhasty disarmament this had to be endured, even at the cost of much indignity. But there is no reason why it should be tolerated indefinitely. "It is my expectation," said Senator Vandenberg, in a letter to a correspondent, "that when some paramount issue (let us say like atomic energy) flatly divides the United Nations, it may well happen that those of us who are in agreement in the United Nations separate ourselves from those who are in disagreement."

This is not cited in order to advocate this course of action either now or at the moment of the Revising Assembly. It is mentioned only as an answer to those who see no way out of the apparent present *impasse*. It is *not* an *impasse*. There is more than one way out. What is essential is that the free peoples should stay together and move forward together, subordinating their individual interests and even their individual grievances, when this is necessary, to the common welfare. Only so will mankind reach the state of inner tranquillity which is the essence of true peace.

NOTES

NOTES

These Notes are printed separately since the text was written to be read continuously and it was not wished to divert the reader's attention by notes at the foot of the page or by numerals pointing to the end of the book. Some of the Notes are simply references to books the use of which it would have been ill-mannered not to acknowledge: others are explanations and, in a few cases, comments, on points where the text may have left a question mark in some readers' minds.

CHAPTER 1

In the brief analysis of Mackinder's ideas and outlook in the text, account has been taken not only of the 1904 lecture but also of his geography lectures at Oxford during the same period, of which the writer has a clear recollection. Much of the substance of these was embodied in a book, *Democratic Ideas and Reality*, published in 1919 and republished in the United States in 1942. See also the prescient concluding paragraph of *Britain and the British Seas*, published in 1902. Mackinder's final pronouncement was an article contributed to *Foreign Affairs* in July, 1943. In this he analyzed the concept of the Heartland in greater detail, describing it as "the greatest natural fortress on earth." He pointed out, that, broadly speaking, the territory of the U.S.S.R. is equivalent to the Heartland, except in one direction. That exception is the rugged forest-clad country, to the East of the grassland zone, extending from the Yenisei River to the Bering Strait. He called this country "Lenaland," drawing attention to the fact that, as contrasted with Heartland Russia, with its more than 170 million inhabitants, it is very sparsely populated and its rich natural resources as yet virtually undeveloped. At the time when Mackinder wrote, the gold-mining industry in the Dalstroy area, with its horrible system of slave labor, was not yet known in the West. See the map on page 65 of Dallin and Nicolaevsky, *Forced Labor in Soviet Russia* (Yale University Press, 1947).

The American Road to World Peace

CHAPTERS 3 and 4

The free and friendly atmosphere described in the text has not come about of itself but as the fruit of persistent social effort, especially during the last fifty years. Intergroup relations are very different from what they were when Jane Addams started her work among immigrant groups in Chicago early in the century, blazing a trail which many others have followed. See her *Democracy and Social Ethics* (1902) and *New Ideals of Peace* (1907). It would be unfair to omit the outstanding contribution to American integration made by the sociologists, from Sumner, with his concept of *mores*, through Park and Burgess, with their neighborhood studies of Chicago, and Stonequist (*The Marginal Man*, 1937), to Maciver. See, in particular, the classic theoretical work of the last named on *Community* (1917) and his more recent book (1945), *The More Perfect Union: a Program for the Control of Inter-group discrimination in the United States.*

On the intellectual side, the task outlined by Emerson in 1837 has been bravely and persistently carried forward during the last fifty years, in defiance of many confusing cross-currents, by Van Wyck Brooks, especially in his great five-volume series *Makers and Finders: A History of the Writer in America, 1815-1915:* this has been carried on well beyond 1915 and bears directly on the present day. The reader should contrast the conditions described in *America's Coming of Age*, 1914, with the concluding chapter of *The Confident Years*, 1952.

Holmes' definition of Law: see his *Collected Legal Papers* (1920) p. 170.

CHAPTER 6

The "treason" of the intellectuals. The reference is to Benda, *La Trahison des Clercs* (1927). The extenuating circumstances mentioned in the text do not apply to the English-speaking countries, where certain groups of self-styled intellectuals have disgraced themselves during the last generation. In many cases the root cause of this phenomenon, out of which so much literary capital has been made, is to be found, not in "disillusionment with Western democracy" or "despair of Western values" but in personal maladjustments which a good education should have enabled these misguided spirits to master. Does not this provide food for the educators to ponder upon? The inquisitive reader may be referred to *The God that Failed*, by Richard Crossman and others (1949).

"A great English scholar": the allusion is to Lord Acton. He never wrote his long-meditated history of freedom, but the gist of it may be found in two essays, "The History of Freedom in Antiquity" and "The History of Freedom in Christianity" published after his death and recently reprinted in the United States (1948). A more recent British writer, Dr. A. J. Carlyle, in his *Political Liberty* (1941) has traced the *idea* of liberty from classical times to the French Revolution and beyond; but his larger six-volume work on *Political Thought in the West*, fascinating though it is, is *not* a history of the development, or even of the vicissitudes, of constitutional freedom.

Notes

CHAPTER 7

See Pascal, *Pensées*, Article VI, 9, and Montesquieu, *L'Esprit des Lois*, Book III, especially Chapter 2.

CHAPTER 15

Roman Law. See the Chapter by Professor H. D. Hazeltine in the *Cambridge Mediaeval History*, Vol. V, in particular pp. 734-35: for Switzerland see p. 755 and for England, pp. 758-60. See also Shakespeare, *Henry IV*, Part II, Act 3, Scene 2, where the "country justices," Shallow and Silence, exchange reminiscences of their days in the Inns of Court, where the English Common Law was a staple of instruction. See also an article by the present writer in the *Classical Journal*, April, 1951.

CHAPTER 20

International Law. See a paper by the writer in the Transactions of the London Grotius Society, Vol. XX (1934).

CHAPTER 21

See Callender, *The Naval Side of British History* (1924), p. 237.

CHAPTER 22

The leading exponent of the theme that large-scale war in the twentieth century would be foolish as well as wicked was Norman Angell, whose book, first named *Europe's Optical Illusion*, (1909) and then, in an enlarged form *The Great Illusion*, (1910) was widely read in the West. Norman Angell, however, never maintained that, because war would be foolish, it would not take place, though many of his readers jumped to this conclusion. During the immediate prewar years Graham Wallas, a thinker of great stature, published two volumes dealing with the same problem on a deeper level: *Human Nature in Politics* (1908) and *The Great Society*, published in the first half of 1914.

Definition of the sentiment of nationality: The reference is to the writer's essay on this subject, printed in the *Sociological Review*, Vol. VIII (Oct. 1915), reprinted with other essays (including one on the menace of the Bolshevik revolution) in *Nationality and Government* (1918). See also on this subject Macartney, *National States and National Minorities* (1934), *La Nationalité et l'histoire*, ed: Koht, Paris 1929, bulletin of the International Committee of Historical Sciences (with special reference to Norway), and Carlton J. H. Hayes, *Essays on Nationalism* (1926). At that time and indeed right up to World War II political nationalism was looked upon by most Western political thinkers as a specifically European phenomenon and hardly anyone had considered the problems which would arise if it became a prominent issue in Asia—not to say Africa.

CHAPTER 24

Masaryk and *Huber*. The clearest exposition by Professor (later President) Masaryk in English is his inaugural lecture as Professor of Central and East European Studies in King's College, London, in 1915 under the title: "The Small Nations in the European Crisis." A fuller statement was printed for private circulation at that time. The collected works of Max Huber, a former President of the Permanent Court of International Justice, have been published at Zurich in three volumes, of which the third (1948) contains his writings on international subjects, including the memorable essay modestly entitled: "Contributions to the Understanding of the Sociological Foundations of the Law of Nations and Society of States," published in 1910 and reprinted in 1928.

CHAPTER 26

Conference on shipboard. See *The Intimate Papers of Colonel House*, Vol. IV, chapter 9.

CHAPTER 30

Mercantile Republic. See Adam Smith, *The Wealth of Nations*, Book IV, chapter 1. For the projected International Trade Organization, see Clair Wilcox, *A Charter for World Trade* (1949) and his letter to *The New York Times*, November 24, 1952.

CHAPTER 32

The view taken on the question of disarmament in this chapter has been confirmed, as these Notes are being corrected for the press, by President Eisenhower in his Inaugural Address, where he speaks of the "joint effort to remove the causes of mutual fears and distrust among nations" as the means necessary in order "to make possible the drastic reduction of armaments."

CHAPTER 34

The "shift in policy:" See Stimson and Bundy, *On Active Service in Peace and War*, pp. 184-85. For the reference to Professor William Rappard see his book, *International Relations Viewed from Geneva* (1925), p. 103.

CHAPTER 35

The Jurists' Tribunal. See Jessup, *Elihu Root*, I, 938, chapter 46.

Advisory Opinions; the practice of seeking these seems likely to play an important part in the development of the United Nations. For its origin in England, its adoption in the constitution of Massachusetts (1780), then in the constitutions of New Hampshire, Maine, Rhode Island, Missouri (but later dropped), Florida, Colorado, South Dakota, Delaware, and Alabama, see Hudson, *The Permanent Court of International Justice* (1925), pp. 141 ff.

CHAPTER 39

"That extraordinary movement," Lippmann, *United States Foreign Policy*, 1943, p. 58. For the racial equality discussions in Paris, which bore such bitter fruit, see Seymour, *The Intimate Papers of Colonel House*, Vol. IV (1928), 309 ff. and the first-hand account of the crucial discussion in Miller, *The Drafting Of the Covenant*, I, 461 ff, also II, 702-4, the Japanese protest in Plenary Session.

"1923 loomed ahead," Bemis, *A Diplomatic History of the United States* (1937), p. 688, of which further use is made in this chapter.

President Harding's Senate address: the extract cited in the text has been taken from the official volume published at the close of the conference.

"*Already on September 21*." New light has recently been thrown on these events from the angle of the Geneva authorities, perhaps too much concerned for the "prestige" of the League, in Walters, *A History of the League of Nations*, II (1952), 465 ff. From the account there given no one could guess that the Washington Treaties had as direct a bearing on the Japanese aggression as the Covenant of the League of Nations. See also Griswold, *The Far Eastern Policy of the United States* (1938), p. 411.

"Each new Japanese aggression." See Stimson and Bundy, *On Active Service in Peace and War*, 1940, pp. 232 ff.

CHAPTER 40

"Baulked idealism:" This expression is a characteristic product of the thought of Graham Wallas.

"For ever and for ever." See Hunter Miller, *The Peace Pact of Paris* (1928).

CHAPTER 41

"Greatly annoyed the Soviet authorities." See Stimson, *op. cit.* pp. 188-89.

"The incalculable harm:" Stimson, pp. 234 ff.

Last paragraph of chapter: The view here taken differs sharply from the skillful presentation of the subject by C. P. Fitzgerald, *Revolution in China* (London, 1952). Mr. Fitzgerald, who resided in Peking from 1946 to 1950 and who is now Reader in Far Eastern History in the Australian National University, does not seem to have added political science to his equipment as a historian, since he describes himself as "a philosophical anarchist" and as holding the view that "all governments are bad and some are worse." He is thus a historian without a

Notes

standard of values. Since he apparently left China in 1950, he was not on the spot when the movement which he so cold-bloodedly describes produced its inevitable fruits in wholesale violence and "liquidations."

There is a very life-like and revealing account of Mao Tse-Tung, as he was in 1934, by a former Peruvian Communist who took part, as a privileged visitor, in a private conference of the Chinese Communist delegation to Moscow in that year. Mao's most marked trait at that time was his subservience to Stalin. See *The Yenan Way* by Eudocio Ravines, New York 1951, pp. 149 ff.

CHAPTER 42

"An avalanche of isolationism:" *Memoirs* of Cordell Hull, p. 399. *Dead level of neutral conduct: In Active Service*, p. 312.

CHAPTER 43

Constant use has been made of the *Memoirs* of Cordell Hull, especially chapters 18, 26, and 37.

CHAPTER 44

On the incidents related in this chapter see Jessup, *International Security*, 1935, pp. 64 ff.

CHAPTER 45

"Functionalism," as an aberration in political theory, has a considerable history. In France it took the form of "Syndicalism," i.e. Labor Unionism, often associated with the idea of a social revolution; in this form it gave rise to the "Soviet" system, so soon to be transformed into its opposite, a totalitarian state.

CHAPTER 46

Hitler's peace offer. See Winston Churchill, *The Gathering Storm* (1948), pp. 484-85.

CHAPTER 47

For the incidents in the first part of this chapter see Winston Churchill, *The Grand Alliance*, (1950) pp. 176 ff. In the latter part use has been made of *Together* by Katherine Marshall (1946).

CHAPTER 48

Atomic Research in Great Britain. See Winston Churchill, *The Grand Alliance*, pp. 814-15.

CHAPTER 51

Stalin's zigzags. See Borkenau, *World-Communism*, 1939. "Fear for his personal safety": for the precautions taken by Molotov on his visit to England in 1942 see Winston Churchill, *The Hinge of Fate*, pp. 326 ff.

Distorted view of the Soviet regime. An instance of this is the way in which the truth about the Katyn massacre was delayed in reaching the public on both sides of the Atlantic.

CHAPTER 52

See *The Way of the Free*, (1951) pp. 126 ff. The quotation from Winston Churchill is from the Fulton speech, which was delivered on March 5, 1946.

Notes

CHAPTER 53

"History will not disclose": Byrnes, *Speaking Frankly* (1947), p. 265. For the quotation from the Congress of 1928 see article by Allen W. Dulles, *Foreign Affairs*, January, 1947, p. 207.

CHAPTER 54

See Winston Churchill, *The Grand Alliance*, pp. 433 ff. Sherwood, *Roosevelt and Hopkins* (1948), pp. 359 ff. and Welles, *Where are we Heading?* (1946), pp. 4 ff.

CHAPTERS 55 and 56

See Cordell Hull's *Memoirs*, pp. 1625 ff.

CHAPTER 57

See Cordell Hull's *Memoirs*, chapters 92 and 93.

CHAPTER 59

The obstacles briefly analyzed in this chapter constitute the main challenge which UNESCO (the United Nations Educational Scientific and Cultural Organization) was established to meet. See the writer's *Learning and Leadership*, 1925, written for the similar organization in the League of Nations, and the *Report on a UNESCO Educational Center* submitted by him to the First UNESCO Conference in 1946.

CHAPTER 60

The Moscow Conference. See Byrnes, *Speaking Frankly*, p. 268. The passage cited at the end of the chapter is on page 312.

CHAPTER 61

On distorted ideas of integrity see Moorehead, *The Traitors* (1952), whose analysis is, however, disappointingly superficial.

Committee membership. See C. W. Eliot. *University Administration*, (1908), p. 3.

CHAPTER 62

The Phillimore Report and the Cecil Plan are printed in Miller, *The Drafting of the Covenant, Vol. II.* For the French plan see the writer's *The League of Nations and the Rule of Law*, 1935, where his memorandum, which he later summarized in the Cecil Plan, is also given (second edition, pp. 187 ff. and 197 ff.)

CHAPTER 63

The constitutional pattern. See K. C. Wheare, *Modern Constitutions* (1952), p. 49.

CHAPTER 64

The legislature. On this subject Woodrow Wilson's *Congressional Government* (1885) remains a classic.

Notes

Brazil's resignation from the League. The account given of this incident in Walters, pp. 318 ff. ignores the deeper dissatisfaction which had been gathering force years before it came out into the open over the Council seat.

CHAPTER 67

The Bruce Report. See Walters, pp. 756 ff., who recalls the encouraging letter written to the Secretary-General on the nonpolitical activities of the League.

CHAPTER 69

See Evatt, *The United Nations* (1948).

CHAPTER 72

The concluding passage about the Secretariat was written before the recent Congressional inquiry and New York Grand Jury presentment, which have underlined the view taken in the text.

CHAPTER 73

The controversy about the nature of arbitration is conveniently summarized in the *United Nations Bulletin* for September 1, 1952.

"A high authority": see Brierly, *The Outlook for International Law*, Oxford 1944, p. 119.

INDEX

INDEX

Index

Index

Index

Index

Index

286

Index

287